AGRICULTURE ISSUES AND POLICIES

AGRICULTURAL TRADE BETWEEN THE U.S. AND CUBA

ISSUES AND PROSPECTS

Agriculture Issues and Policies

Additional books in this series can be found on Nova's website under the Series tab.

Additional e-books in this series can be found on Nova's website under the e-book tab.

AGRICULTURE ISSUES AND POLICIES

AGRICULTURAL TRADE BETWEEN THE U.S. AND CUBA

ISSUES AND PROSPECTS

LANA VALDEZ
EDITOR

nova publishers
New York

Library of Congress Cataloging-in-Publication Data

ISBN: 978-1-63484-430-7

Published by Nova Science Publishers, Inc. † New York

CONTENTS

PREFACE

Amid more than a half a century of antagonistic political relations between the United States and Cuba during which commercial ties were largely severed, U.S. exports of agricultural products to the island nation currently stand out as one of the few points of engagement between the two countries, if to a limited degree. U.S. exports of medicine and medical products is the other product category for which the U.S. government has eased its long-standing embargo on trade with Cuba. In a major diplomatic initiative, President Obama announced in December 2014 a significant shift in relations with Cuba with the goal of transitioning from a decades-long policy of sanctions that were designed to isolate Cuba toward a more normal bilateral relationship. This book reviews the current state of agricultural trade between the United States and Cuba, identifies key impediments to expanding bilateral trade in agricultural products, identifies key provisions in the law to which these obstacles are anchored, and considers the potential consequences for trade in agricultural goods in the event that the current thaw in diplomatic relations was to be extended more broadly so that bilateral trade was returned to a more normal footing. It also summarizes several of the bills introduced in the 114th Congress that propose to remove specific restrictions that impede trade in agricultural goods or that seek to lift the embargo on Cuba entirely. This book also discusses the past, present, and possible future of the U.S.- Cuba agricultural trade; and provides information on Cuba's regulatory environment as it relates to U.S. agricultural exports.

In: Agricultural Trade Between the U.S. and Cuba ISBN: 978-1-63484-430-7
Editor: Lana Valdez

Chapter 1

U.S. AGRICULTURAL TRADE WITH CUBA: CURRENT LIMITATIONS AND FUTURE PROSPECTS*

Mark A. McMinimy

SUMMARY

After more than half a century during which trade relations between the United States and Cuba have evolved from a tight economic embargo to a narrow window of trade in U.S. agricultural and medical products, the diplomatic initiative that President Obama announced in December 2014 to restore more normal relations with Cuba has raised the possibility that bilateral relations could move toward an expansion in commercial opportunities.

Many U.S. agricultural and food industry interests believe the Cuban market could offer meaningful export expansion potential for their products—but only if a number of restrictions under the U.S. embargo on trade with Cuba were to be removed. Among the measures most often cited as inhibiting exports of U.S. products, while simultaneously benefiting foreign competitors, are a prohibition on the provision of private financing and credit on sales to Cuba; denial of access to U.S. government credit guarantees and export promotion programs; the ban on

* This is an edited, reformatted and augmented version of a Congressional Research Service publication R44119, prepared for Members and Committees of Congress, dated October 1, 2015.

general tourism to Cuba; and the general prohibition on U.S. imports of Cuban goods.

Some Members of Congress have introduced legislation in the 114th Congress that would ease U.S. economic sanctions on Cuba. These bills span a broad range of approaches, from a narrow focus on removing the ban on providing private financing and credit for the sale of agricultural goods to Cuba to far broader legislative initiatives that seek to lift the Cuban embargo altogether.

A question that arises for policymakers as diplomatic relations with Cuba are restored is what the potential opportunity is for U.S. food and agricultural exports to Cuba if bilateral relations are returned to a more normal status in the future. Corollary questions are what agricultural products Cuba might export to the United States if the existing prohibition on Cuban products were to be removed, and what implications trade in Cuban products could hold for U.S. agriculture.

Numerous stakeholders within the food and agriculture industry, as well as the U.S. Department of Agriculture (USDA), contend that U.S. agricultural exports to Cuba could expand markedly if key elements of the embargo against Cuba were removed. The prohibition on providing private credit and financing and the ban on access to government export promotion programs are two that are often cited. USDA asserts that basic commodities, like U.S. rice, wheat, dry beans, and dried milk could readily gain market share in Cuba under more normal trade relations in view of the close proximity of U.S. ports to Cuba compared with export competitors. Higher value food and agricultural products might make inroads in Cuba over time, it is argued, particularly if Cuba could increase its access to foreign exchange by selling its products in the United States.

A concern voiced by some in agriculture is that opening the U.S. market to Cuba could pave the way for a new influx of tropical fruit and vegetable products that would compete directly with winter-season production in Florida, particularly if foreign investors perceive the opportunity to create an export platform for the U.S. market in Cuba. Among the concerns raised is that Cuban production is often subsidized by the government; also, that allowing Cuban produce into the U.S. market could become a conduit for introducing new pests and plant diseases. While Cuba was once a leading sugar producer and the largest foreign supplier to the U.S. market prior to the embargo, its sugar industry has undergone a steep decline since the demise of the Soviet Union. Cuba continues to export limited quantities of sugar and might very well request access to the lucrative U.S. sugar market if normal trade relations were restored. But any such opportunity would most likely be the result of a negotiated agreement between the United States and Cuba.

INTRODUCTION

Amid more than a half a century of antagonistic political relations between the United States and Cuba during which commercial ties were largely severed, U.S. exports of agricultural products to the island nation currently stand out as one of the few points of engagement between the two countries, if to a limited degree. U.S. exports of medicine and medical products is the other product category for which the U.S. government has eased its long-standing embargo on trade with Cuba. In a major diplomatic initiative, President Obama announced in December 2014 a significant shift in relations with Cuba with the goal of transitioning from a decades-long policy of sanctions that were designed to isolate Cuba toward a more normal bilateral relationship.

To advance the goal of normalizing relations with Cuba, the President announced a series of actions designed to move the two nations closer to this objective. These included reestablishing diplomatic relations; reviewing the State Department's designation of Cuba as a state sponsor of international terrorism; and providing limited openings for increasing travel, and for expanding commerce and the flow of information. In May 2015, the State Department removed Cuba from the list of state sponsors of terrorism, and on July 20, 2015, the United States and Cuba reestablished diplomatic relations and reopened embassies in their respective capitals. While these actions are tangible steps in the direction of a more normal relationship with Cuba and will ease the embargo in some areas, the majority of economic restrictions first imposed on Cuba in 1962 remain in place.[1]

This report reviews the current state of agricultural trade between the United States and Cuba, identifies key impediments to expanding bilateral trade in agricultural products, identifies key provisions in the law to which these obstacles are anchored, and considers the potential consequences for trade in agricultural goods in the event that the current thaw in diplomatic relations was to be extended more broadly so that bilateral trade was returned to a more normal footing. It also summarizes several of the bills introduced in the 114th Congress that propose to remove specific restrictions that impede trade in agricultural goods or that seek to lift the embargo on Cuba entirely.

Background and Perspective

Relations between the United States and Cuba deteriorated sharply, and then decisively, in the early 1960s following a series of dramatic events that recast the U.S.-Cuba relationship along antagonistic lines. Chief among these events were Fidel Castro's action in the early 1960s to build a repressive communist regime and move Cuba toward close relations with the Soviet Union; the expropriation of U.S. economic assets on the island nation located a mere 90 miles from Florida; U.S. covert operations to overthrow the Castro regime in the failed Bay of Pigs invasion of Cuba in 1961; and the subsequent confrontation between the United States and the Soviet Union over the Kremlin's attempt to install offensive nuclear missiles in Cuba in 1962.

From Embargo and Sanctions to a Window for Farm Exports

In response to these events, President Kennedy imposed an embargo on trade with Cuba in 1962. The trade embargo was subsequently expanded—to prohibit most financial transactions and to freeze Cuban government assets in the United States. The web of U.S. sanctions on Cuba was strengthened in subsequent years and was also broadened to include various democracy-building measures with the enactment of additional laws, including the Cuban Democracy Act (CDA) of 1992 (P.L. 102-484) and the Cuban Liberty and Solidarity (LIBERTAD) Act of 1996 (P.L. 104- 114), the latter frequently referred to as Helms/Burton legislation. In 2000, with passage of P.L. 106-387, the Trade Sanctions Reform and Export Enhancement Act of 2000 (TSRA), Congress opened the door to U.S. agricultural exports to Cuba, but with restrictions on credit and financing.

Obstacles Impeding U.S. Agricultural Exports to Cuba

The U.S. sanctions regime against Cuba has been tweaked in various ways in the years since TSRA was enacted, but alterations have been mostly at the edges, and this continues to be the case. Notwithstanding the new diplomatic opening to Cuba that President Obama unveiled late last year in tandem with his expressed desire to move toward a more normal relationship with Cuba, key restrictions on economic relations with Cuba persist. Among the plethora of restrictions that remain in place, those frequently identified as suppressing trade in U.S. products to Cuba include the following:

- a prohibition on the provision of credit and financing for U.S. exports;
- denial of access to government programs and commercial facilities that otherwise would be available to promote and facilitate U.S. agricultural exports to Cuba;
- the ban on general U.S. tourism to Cuba; and
- a general ban on U.S. imports of goods from Cuba, with a recently introduced exception for goods produced by Cuban entrepreneurs.

USDA Identifies Key Barriers to Expanded Agriculture Exports to Cuba

That significant barriers continue to restrict the potential for U.S. agricultural exports to Cuba was acknowledged recently by the U.S. Department of Agriculture (USDA) in April 2015 testimony before the Senate Agriculture Committee. USDA asserted that if the embargo were removed, the United States could become "a major trading partner with Cuba," considering that Cuba imports around 80% of its food and that U.S. exporters enjoy significant logistical advantages over their major export competitors in Brazil and Europe.[2] But it contends that these potential advantages are more than offset by a number of policies governing food and agricultural exports to Cuba, pointing to the prohibition on any U.S. government export assistance under TSRA, such as credit guarantees and market promotion programs, as one. Among impediments to expanding U.S. agricultural exports to Cuba that are not governed by the embargo, USDA cited Cuba's limited supply of foreign exchange and its requirement that all U.S. imports be funneled through Cuba's state corporation, Alimport—a requirement that is not imposed on all of Cuba's suppliers.

Subsequently, in a report of June 2015 on the potential for U.S.-Cuba agricultural trade, USDA's Economic Research Service cites restrictions imposed by TSRA on the terms of payments and financing as a "major inhibitor of U.S. agricultural exports to Cuba."[3] Under TSRA, payment or financing terms are limited to either cash in advance or financing by third-country financial institutions, with the latter being a more laborious process than making a conventional payment directly from the buyer's financial institution in Cuba to the seller's financial institution in the United States. Following President Obama's "normalization" initiative in late 2014, the U.S. Treasury altered its interpretation of "cash in advance" from one that required cash payment before the shipment of goods from a U.S. port of departure to one that requires cash payment before transfer of title. Moreover, U.S. institutions also were allowed to open correspondent accounts at Cuban financial institutions. Still, in its Cuba report of June 2015, USDA concludes that lacking the ability to extend credit to Cuban buyers places U.S. agricultural exporters at a competitive disadvantage in relation to other exporting countries.

U.S. Agricultural Interests Offer Perspective on Trade with Cuba

In December 2014, the Senate Committee on Finance requested that the U.S. International Trade Commission (USITC) conduct an investigation and issue a report on trends in Cuban imports of goods and services, including from the United States. The Committee also requested that the agency provide an analysis of U.S. restrictions affecting Cuba's purchases. In its letter to USITC, the committee identified three areas of particular interest:

- an overview of Cuba's imports of goods and services from, to the extent possible, 2005 to the present, including identification of major supplying countries, products, and market segments;
- a description of how U.S. restrictions on trade, including those relating to export financing terms and travel to Cuba by U.S. citizens, affect Cuban imports of U.S. goods and services; and
- for sectors where the impact is likely to be significant, a qualitative and, to the extent possible, quantitative estimate of U.S. exports of goods and services to Cuba, in the event that statutory, regulatory, or other trade restrictions on U.S. exports of goods and services as well as travel to Cuba by U.S. citizens are lifted.

In response to the Finance Committee's request, USITC held a hearing in June 2015 to solicit the views of a range of experts and interested stakeholders. At that hearing, a number of witnesses with agricultural trade interests specifically cited the restriction on the provision of credit as a particular handicap for U.S. agricultural exporters. For instance, testimony provided by Cargill, Inc. asserted that "Cuba is still importing food, but is choosing our competitors as suppliers more often than not."[4] Cargill listed seven challenges that U.S. agricultural exporters face in the Cuban market:

1. restrictions on financing that make U.S. exporters uncompetitive;
2. a cumbersome payment process that stems from the financing restrictions;

3. travel difficulties facing Cuban importers who wish to observe vessel loadings;
4. inability to offer price risk tools to Cuba due to U.S. financing restrictions;
5. lack of consultations between U.S. and Cuban government regulatory officials;
6. inability to invest in Cuban agriculture and food sectors; and
7. the ban on U.S. tourism to Cuba, which constrains high-value, tourist-oriented U.S. food exports.

In its testimony to USITC, Riceland Foods, Inc., a farmer-owned cooperative and direct exporter of U.S. rice and wheat, cited key actions the U.S. government would need to take in order for U.S. producers to regain market share in rice in Cuba that has been lost as a result of the trade embargo:

- remove the ban on U.S. tourist travel to Cuba;
- allow direct banking services and the extension of credit on commercial terms; and
- permit Cuba to export its goods to the United States.

Also offering testimony before USITC was an agricultural economist from with the University of Florida, who pointed out that sales of U.S. intermediate and consumer-oriented foods have held up fairly well amid the overall decline in sales of U.S. agricultural product sales to Cuba in recent years, whereas bulk grains have borne the brunt of the loss of market share to non-U.S. suppliers.[5] He cited the credit provided by export competitors and the inability of U.S. exporters to be competitive on this element of a sale as the single most important factor in Cuba's shift away from U.S. rice.

USITC's report on Cuba imports and the effects of U.S. restrictions on U.S. exports to that country was expected to be transmitted to the Committee on Finance on September 15, 2015,[6] but on August 19, 2015, the committee asked USITC to expand the scope of its investigation and rescheduled the report's due date for March 17, 2016.[7] The request adds the following elements:

- A qualitative analysis of existing Cuban non-tariff measures, Cuban institutional and infrastructural factors, and other Cuban barriers that would inhibit U.S. and non-U.S. firms in conducting business in and with Cuba, among which: restrictions on trade and investment;

property rights and ownership; customs duties and procedures; sanitary and phytosanitary measures; state trading; protection of intellectual property rights; and infrastructure affecting telecommunications, port facilities, and the storage, transport, and distribution of goods;

- A qualitative analysis of any effects that such measures, factors, and barriers would have on U.S. exports of goods and services to Cuba in the event of changes to statutory, regulatory, or other trade restrictions on U.S. exports of goods and services to Cuba; and
- To the extent feasible, a quantitative analysis of the aggregate effects of Cuban tariff and non-tariff measures on the ability of U.S. and non-U.S. firms to conduct business in and with Cuba.

USITC has extended the deadline for written submissions to October 23, 2015.

U.S. Agricultural Trade with Cuba over the Years

Prior to the Cuban revolution in 1959 that brought Castro to power and triggered the deterioration in U.S.-Cuban relations, the United States and Cuba conducted a brisk trade in agricultural products. During the three fiscal years before the revolution—FY1956-1958—Cuba ranked as the ninth largest market for U.S. agricultural exports and the second largest supplier of U.S. agricultural imports, according to the U.S. Department of Agriculture (USDA). In a report issued in June 2015, the agency notes that rice, lard, pork, and wheat flour led the list of U.S. farm exports to Cuba in value terms, with Cuba ranking as the largest foreign market for U.S. long-grain rice. Cane sugar, molasses, tobacco, and coffee topped the list of U.S. agricultural imports from Cuba during that period.[8] With the advent of the Castro regime and the imposition of U.S. sanctions, U.S. agricultural trade with Cuba ground to a halt in the early 1960s.

Trade in farm products remained at a standstill until Congress enacted the Trade Sanctions Reform and Export Enhancement Act of 2000 (P.L. 106-387), or TSRA, which authorized certain sales of food, medicines, and medical equipment to a number of countries, including Cuba. TSRA did not change the general ban on imports from Cuba, including agricultural products, and it added prohibitions on extending credit to facilitate agricultural sales to Cuba and on providing any U.S. government support for exports to Cuba.

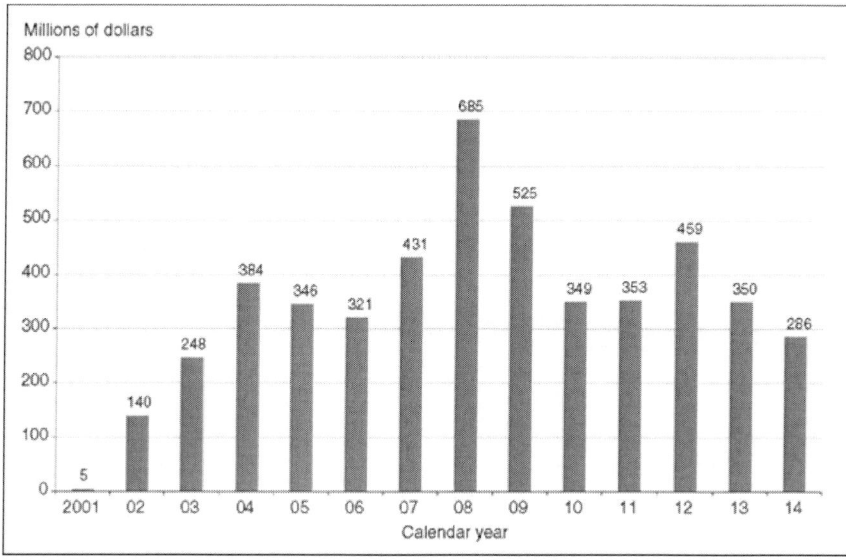

Source: U.S. Department of Agriculture Foreign Agricultural Service.

Figure 1. U.S. Agricultural Exports to Cuba (2001-2014).

Notwithstanding these disadvantages, U.S. agricultural exporters quickly established a foothold in Cuba, with export sales reaching a peak of $685 million in calendar year (CY) 2008 in the aftermath of several hurricanes and tropical storms (*Figure 1*), representing 0.6% of total U.S. agricultural exports of $114.8 billion that year.

The level of U.S. agricultural exports to Cuba has trended lower since 2008, averaging $365 million a year during the most recent three calendar years, from 2012 to 2014, or about 0.25% of average U.S. agricultural exports to the world of $145.4 billion over this period. Most recently, U.S. agricultural exports to Cuba dipped to $286 million in CY2014. A parallel trend is that U.S. exports to Cuba have become increasingly concentrated in a few commodities, with chicken meat (leg quarters), corn, soybean meal, and soybeans accounting for 84% of the total between 2012 and 2014 (*Table 1*).

A number of close observers have suggested the decline in U.S. food and agricultural exports to Cuba in recent years is likely the product of several factors, among which are a preference within the Cuban government for diversifying its supplier network; an effort to establish closer relations with certain allies, such as China and Vietnam; and the availability of credit offered by some nonU.S. suppliers that U.S. competitors are prevented from providing under the U.S. trade sanctions regime.[9] Concerning the role of credit, USDA asserts that “U.S. restrictions on extending credit to Cuban buyers have made it harder for U.S. agricultural exporters to sell a larger volume and broader variety of commodities to Cuba.”[10]

Table 1. Major U.S. Agricultural Product Exports to Cuba

	2012-2014 Average	
Product	Value, $1,000	Percent of Total
Total Agricultural Exports	365.3	100%
- Animals and Products	161.2	
—Chicken meat	148.9	41%
—Pork	4.3	1.2%
- Grains and Feeds	97.3	
—Corn	72.9	20%
—Brewing/distilling dregs	14.1	3.9%
—Mixed feeds	10.3	2.8%
- Oilseeds and Products	103.5	
—Soybean meal	59.4	16.3%
—Soybeans	44.1	12.1%

Source: U.S. Department of Agriculture, Foreign Agricultural Service.
Note: Totals do not add up because list is limited to major products.

Figure 2 illustrates that as Cuba’s agricultural imports from the United States have fallen in recent years, Cuba has increased its imports from the rest of the world, with the European Union and Brazil ranking as Cuba’s largest suppliers in CY2014.

Potential for Expanded Agricultural Trade with Cuba

A number of the witnesses at the USITC hearing asserted that the Cuba market offers potential growth opportunities for U.S. food and agricultural exports, a view that was underscored in the USDA report of June 2015.[11] Sounding a cautionary note on the topic of liberalizing trade with Cuba was the University of Florida economist, who cited concerns about potential threats to Florida agriculture that could be realized if the ban on imports from Cuba were to be lifted.

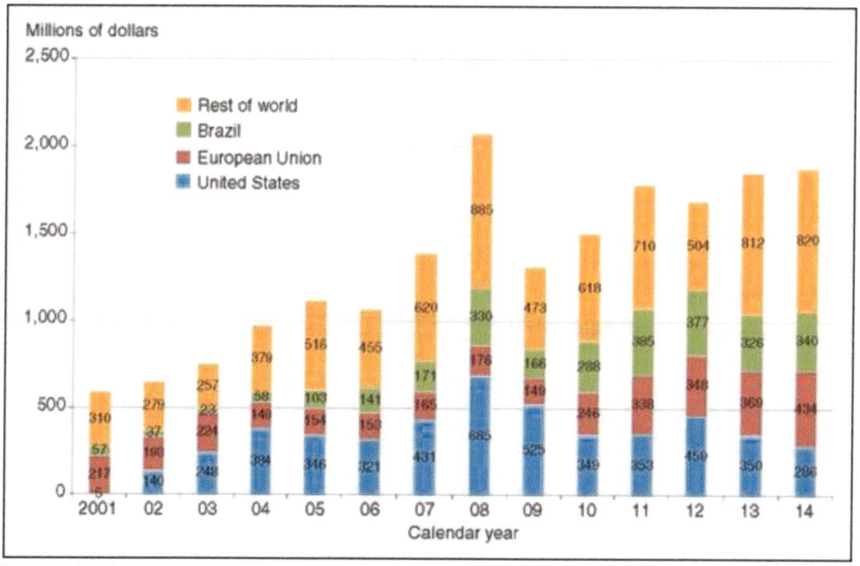

Source: U.S. Department of Agriculture.

Figure 2. Cuba's Agricultural Imports by Origin, 2001-2014 (2001-2014).

In its June 2015 report on the potential for increased U.S. agricultural trade with Cuba, USDA points to several important similarities between Cuba and the Dominican Republic, including population size and per capita income in terms of purchasing power parity. Given these similarities, the report goes on to consider whether the Cuban market for U.S. agricultural exports, which averaged $365 million from 2012-2014, might have the potential to expand to a level closer to that of the Dominican Republic, which absorbed an average of $1.1 billion of U.S. agricultural products over the same three years. USDA cites Cuba's close geographic proximity to the United States as a potential advantage for U.S. food and agricultural product exports that could help to drive export gains. Another reason that the agency sees an opportunity to expand U.S. agricultural product exports to Cuba is that the U.S. share of the market in Cuba, at about 20%, is less than half the U.S. market share in the Dominican Republic.

A Possible Market Opportunity for U.S. Rice

In terms of product mix, USDA sees the potential for U.S. rice to "regain a large share of Cuba's import market," if a normal trading relationship were to be established—but only if U.S. suppliers are allowed to provide competitive terms of credit. Among the advantages that favor U.S. rice compared with rice from current suppliers Vietnam and Brazil are the year-round availability of high-quality rice that Cuban consumers prefer, and transportation cost advantages. USDA suggests that exports of other U.S. commodities that have flagged in recent years, such as dry beans, wheat, and dry milk, could also rebound if normal trade relations were restored. In addition, USDA contends that tourist-oriented food service sales could support U.S. exports of cheese; yogurt; and higher value cuts of pork, poultry meat, and beef, particularly if restrictions on tourism to Cuba were relaxed. The agency also sees potential for expanded U.S. export sales of low-value cuts of pork, pork variety meats, chicken leg quarters, and milk powder, subject to further income growth within Cuba. In recent years, Cuba has imported significant quantities of wheat, rice, and nonfat dried milk (*Figure 3*), but almost all of this trade accrued to non-U.S. suppliers.

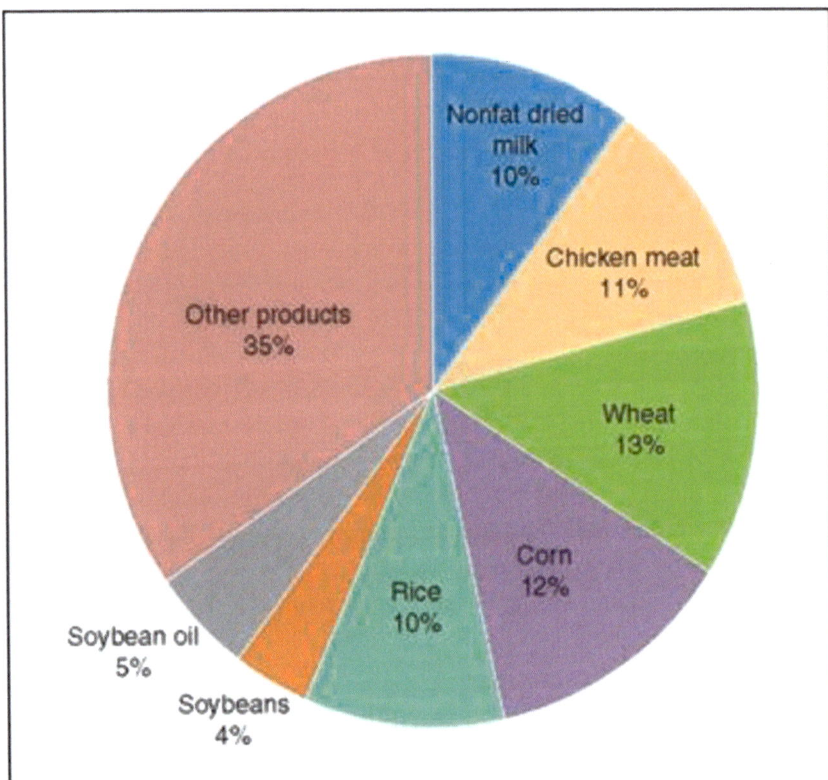

Source: U.S. Department of Agriculture.

Figure 3. Composition of Cuba's Agricultural Imports (2012-2014).

2014/2015 with exports averaging just below 1 million tons annually. (*Figure 4*).

Cuban Sugar Exports and the U.S. Market

Given Cuba's resource endowments and history as a major sugar producer, Cuba might expand its output and exports with additional investments. Although the United States is the world's largest sugar importer and Cuba was the largest foreign source of sugar for the U.S. market prior to the U.S. embargo, any post-embargo access to the U.S. sugar market would have to be negotiated. Any such access might well be quite limited in scope given the existing limitations on sugar imports under the U.S. sugar program via tariff rate quotas (TRQs), free-trade agreements, and through a 2014 export limitation agreement with Mexico.[17] The United States currently provides low- or no-duty access to most of its supplier countries based on historical trade patterns as determined under an agreement struck under the auspices of the World Trade Organization.

In its June 2015 study, USDA concluded, "A more normal trading relationship with Cuba would likely result in the establishment of some U.S. sugar imports from Cuba, but at volumes much smaller than during the late 1950s." USDA cites a 2002 paper authored by two officials at the U.S. International Trade Commission that identifies six possible options for providing Cuba with access to the U.S. sugar market that the authors contend would be compliant with the existing multilateral trade agreements at the World Trade Organization (WTO):[18]

- allocate WTO quotas on a first-come, first-serve basis;
- auction sugar quotas;
- redistribute the tariff-rate quota (TRQ) among countries, including Cuba;
- increase the TRQ to accommodate Cuba;
- replace the existing TRQ with a simple tariff; and
- provide market access for sugar as part of a free trade agreement with Cuba.

Legislative Initiatives Aimed at Easing Restrictions on U.S. Agricultural Exports to Cuba

When President Obama announced his initiative to alter the course of U.S.-Cuba relations late last year, he indicated that he does not have the authority to end the embargo because it is codified in legislation. Under the LIBERTAD Act, the President would be required to end the trade embargo if he determines that Cuba has elected a government under free and fair elections and has met other criteria, among which are showing respect for basic civil liberties and human rights of Cuban citizens and Cuba moving to establish a free market economic system. Otherwise, congressional action would be required to end it, either by amending or repealing the LIBERTAD Act and other embargo-related statutes. The text box below identifies existing statutes that contain restrictions that are of particular importance for trade in food and agricultural products with Cuba.

Recognizing that U.S. farmers and exporters are competing for food and agricultural markets in Cuba under terms that place them at a distinct disadvantage compared with foreign competitors that are not subject to restrictions under the U.S. embargo, some Members of Congress have proposed legislation that would ease various elements of the U.S. economic embargo on Cuba, or repeal it entirely. A brief review of several of the legislative initiatives that address agricultural aspects of the trade embargo against Cuba follows.[19]

- Three bills would lift the overall embargo: H.R. 274 (Rush), H.R. 403 (Rangel), and H.R. 735 (Serrano).
- H.R. 635 (Rangel), among its various provisions, has the goal of facilitating the export of U.S. agricultural and medical exports to Cuba by permanently redefining the term "payment of cash in advance" to mean that payment is received before the transfer of title and release and control of the commodity to the purchaser; authorizing direct transfers between Cuban and U.S. financial institutions for products exported under the terms of TSRA; establishing an export promotion program for U.S. agricultural exports to Cuba; and prohibiting restrictions on travel to Cuba.
- S. 491 (Klobuchar) would remove various provisions of law restricting trade and other relations with Cuba, including certain

restrictions in the CDA, the LIBERTAD Act, and TSRA that currently prohibit financing of agricultural sales to Cuba, U.S. export assistance for sales to Cuba including credit and guarantees, and the entry of Cuban goods into the United States.

- S. 1049 (Heitkamp) would amend TSRA to allow for the private financing of agricultural commodity sales to Cuba.
- S. 1543 (Moran) would repeal or amend various provisions of law restricting trade and other relations with Cuba, including certain restrictions in the CDA, the LIBERTAD Act, and TSRA. It would repeal restrictions on private financing for Cuba in TSRA but continue to prohibit U.S. government foreign assistance or financial assistance, loans, loan guarantee, extension of credit, or other financing for export to Cuba, albeit with presidential waiver authority for national security or humanitarian reasons. Under the initiative, the federal government would be prohibited from expending any funds to promote trade with Cuba or develop markets in Cuba, although certain federal commodity research and promotion programs that are funded through mandatory assessments would be allowed.

Select Statutory Provisions Relevant to U.S. Food and Agricultural Exports to Cuba

- Two restrictions that some have identified as being among the most significant in terms of inhibiting U.S. agricultural exports to Cuba are found in Sec. 908 of TSRA (U.S.C. 7207):
  1) prohibiting U.S. aid to facilitate exports to Cuba;
  2) limiting the means by which a U.S. person may finance the sale of agricultural products to Cuba to cash in advance or third-country financing.
- Concerning sugar specifically, section 902 of P.L. 106-387, the Food Security Act of 1985 (U.S.C. 1446 note), denies a sugar import quota to Cuba and to any third country trading in Cuban sugar, although this restriction is subject to presidential waiver under terms provided in the LIBERTAD Act.
- The statutory ban on general tourism to Cuba is in Sec. 910(b) of TSRA (22 U.S.C. 7208(b)).

End Notes

[1] For more on U.S. relations with Cuba see CRS Report R43926, Cuba: Issues for the 114th Congress, by Mark P. Sullivan; CRS Report IF10045, Cuba: President Obama's New Policy Approach, by Mark P. Sullivan; CRS Report R43888, Cuba Sanctions: Legislative Restrictions Limiting the Normalization of Relations, by Dianne E. Rennack and Mark P. Sullivan; and CRS Report RL31139, Cuba: U.S. Restrictions on Travel and Remittances, by Mark P. Sullivan.

[2] Testimony of Michael T. Scuse on April 21, 2015, at http://www.ag.senate.gov/hearings/opportunities-andchallenges-for-agriculture-trade-with-cuba.

[3] U.S.-Cuba Agricultural Trade: Past, Present, and Possible Future, USDA, ERS, June 2015, at http://www.ers.usda.gov/media/1856299/aes87.pdf.

[4] Testimony of Devry Boughner Volwerk, vice president corporate affairs, Cargill, Inc. and chair of the U.S. Agricultural Coalition for Cuba, at http://www.usitc.gov/press_room/spotlight/overview_cuban_imports_goods_and_services_and.htm.

[5] Testimony of William A. Messina, Jr., University of Florida, to the USITC on June 2, 2015, at http://www.usitc.gov/press_room/spotlight/overview_cuban_imports_goods_and_services_and.htm.

[6] For USITC announcement and background, see http://www.usitc.gov/documents/332_ 552_notice01292015sgl.pdf.

[7] Federal Register Notice, September 10, 2015, at http://www.gpo.gov/fdsys/pkg/FR-2015-09-10/pdf/2015-22697.pdf.

[8] U.S.-Cuba Agricultural Trade: Past, Present, and Possible Future, USDA Economic Research Service, at http://www.ers.usda.gov/media/1856299/aes87.pdf.

[9] See testimony of C. Parr Rosson III, Texas A&M University, on June 2, 2015, before the Senate Agriculture Committee at http://www.ag.senate.gov/hearings/opportunities-and-challenges-for-agriculture-trade-with-cuba; also, testimony of William A. Messina, Jr., University of Florida, on June 2, 2015, before the U.S. International Trade Commission at http://www.usitc.gov/press_room/spotlight/overview_cuban_imports_goods_and_services_and.htm.

[10] U.S.-Cuba Agricultural Trade: Past, Present, and Possible Future, USDA Economic Research Service, at http://www.ers.usda.gov/media/1856299/aes87.pdf.

[11] Testimony of witnesses on this topic before the U.S. International Trade Commission is available at http://www.usitc.gov/press_room/spotlight/overview_cuban_ imports_goods_and_services_and.htm.

[12] Testimony of Terry L. Harris, Riceland Foods, Inc. on June 2, 2015, at http://www.usitc.gov/press_room/spotlight/overview_cuban_imports_goods_and_services_and.htm.

[13] Testimony of Marco A. Palma, Texas A&M University, to USITC at http://www.usitc.gov/press_room/spotlight/overview_cuban_imports_goods_and_services_and.htm.

[14] See testimony of William A. Messina, Jr., University of Florida, before the USITC, June 2, 2015, at http://www.usitc.gov/press_room/spotlight/overview_cuban_imports_goods_ and_services_and.htm.

[15] Ibid.

[16] U.S.-Cuba Agricultural Trade: Past, Present, and Possible Future, USDA, ERS, at http://www.ers.usda.gov/media/1856299/aes87.pdf.

[17] For background on the structure and operation of the U.S. sugar program, see CRS Report IF10223, Fundamentals of the U.S. Sugar Program, by Mark A. McMinimy and CRS Report R43998, U.S. Sugar Program Fundamentals, by Mark A. McMinimy.

[18] Normalizing Trade Relations with Cuba: GATT-Compliant Options for the Allocation of the U.S. Sugar Tariff-Rate Quota, Devry S. Boughner and Jonathan R. Coleman, U.S. International Trade Commission, at http://ageconsearch.umn.edu/bitstream/23911/1/03010046.pdf.

[19] For a more comprehensive list of legislation introduced into the 114th Congress to remove trade sanctions on Cuba, see CRS Report R43926, Cuba: Issues for the 114th Congress, by Mark P. Sullivan.

In: Agricultural Trade Between the U.S. and Cuba ISBN: 978-1-63484-430-7
Editor: Lana Valdez

Chapter 2

U.S.-CUBA AGRICULTURAL TRADE: PAST, PRESENT, AND POSSIBLE FUTURE*

Steven Zahniser, Bryce Cooke, Jerry Cessna, Nathan Childs, David Harvey, Mildred Haley, Michael McConnell and Carlos Arnade

ABSTRACT

Establishment of a more normal economic relationship with Cuba has the potential to foster additional growth in U.S.-Cuba agricultural trade. Prior to the Cuban Revolution of 1959, bilateral agricultural trade featured large volumes of Cuban sugar and smaller volumes of molasses, tobacco, and pineapple from Cuba and rice, lard, dried beans, wheat, and wheat flour from the United States. In 2000, the U.S. economic embargo on Cuba was loosened to allow for U.S. exports of agricultural products and medicine. As a result, the United States soon became Cuba's leading supplier of agricultural imports. The remaining prohibitions on issuing credit to Cuba, however, give other exporting countries a competitive advantage in the Cuban market, and the United States slipped to being the second leading supplier in 2013 and the third leading supplier in 2014. A more normal economic relationship between the two countries would allow Cuba to resume exporting agricultural products to the United States, while U.S. agricultural exporters would be able to develop

---

* This is an edited, reformatted and augmented version of research report number AES-87, issued by the U.S. Department of Agriculture, Economic Research Service, June 2015.

commercial ties in Cuba that approximate their business relationships in other parts of the world.

Keywords: Cuba, United States, agricultural trade, embargo, normal trade relations

Introduction

Establishment of a more normal economic relationship with Cuba offers the potential to generate further growth in U.S.-Cuba trade; to foster greater productivity in the Cuban economy; to increase demand for agricultural imports among Cuban consumers, foodservice providers, and food manufacturers; and to allow for the resumption of U.S. agricultural imports from Cuba. Over the past 6 months, the United States and Cuba have taken several small steps toward normalizing their economic relationship. In December 2014, the United States announced that it would begin discussions to re-establish diplomatic relations with Cuba and that it would implement executive actions designed to ease the restrictions on trade, remittances, and travel with Cuba. These executive actions build upon similar measures taken in 2009. However, under current legislation, substantial modifications to the embargo require congressional action.[1]

U.S.-Cuba Trade Once Substantial

Past levels of U.S.-Cuba agricultural trade suggest the possible size and composition of future trade flows between the two countries. Before the Cuban Revolution, the United States and Cuba were major agricultural trading partners. During fiscal years (FY) 1956-58,[2] Cuba was the ninth leading destination for U.S. agricultural exports and the second leading supplier of U.S. agricultural imports. U.S. agricultural exports to Cuba averaged $139 million per year during this period (table 1), while corresponding imports averaged $408 million (table 2), with both figures measured in nominal dollars. At current prices (calendar years 2012-14), U.S. agricultural exports to Cuba during FY 1956-58 would amount to roughly $600 million annually, while U.S. imports from Cuba would equal about $2.2 billion. The large value of U.S. agricultural imports from Cuba during FY 1956- 58, as measured in 2012-14 prices, is due mainly to the sizable volume of sugar imports during that period and the fact that the nominal unit value for U.S. sugar imports increased by about 400 percent between 1956-58 and 2012-14.

Rice, lard, pork, and wheat flour were the four leading U.S. agricultural exports to Cuba in terms of value during FY 1956-58. Cuba was typically the largest commercial market for U.S. long-grain rice exports prior to the embargo, often taking more than half of U.S. annual long-grain sales and almost one-third of total U.S. rice exports (Efferson, 1952: 518-521; USDA, Agricultural Marketing Service, 1956: 16). If Cuba imported the same amount of rice today as it did then, it would be the 7th leading destination for U.S. rice exports, even though Cuba's annual per capita rice consumption was about two-thirds of what it is today.[3] Consumers in pre-revolutionary Cuba generally liked the taste, appearance, and cooking qualities of U.S. rice varieties and were willing to pay a premium for them. Virtually all U.S. rice exports to Cuba prior to the embargo consisted of milled, southern long-grain rice; long-grain rice is still the dominant class of U.S. rice grown for export.[4]

Cane sugar, molasses, tobacco, and coffee were the four leading U.S. agricultural imports from Cuba during FY 1956-58.[5] Past volumes of U.S. sugar imports from Cuba alone (2.8 million metric tons per year) rival contemporary volumes of total U.S. sugar imports from all countries (3.1 million metric tons per year during 2012-14) (table 2). Cuban sugar exports to the United States are unlikely to return to the levels of the late 1950s. Nonetheless, these exports were so vital to the Cuban economy of the 1950s that Dye and Sicotte (2004) posit that a 1956 revision to U.S. sugar trade policy tightening the import quota for Cuba greatly weakened the Cuban economy just as the Revolution was getting underway.

U.S.-Cuba relations quickly deteriorated after Cuba's new government took power. Cuba expropriated U.S. economic assets, including farms and sugar mills, as part of its efforts to institute a socialist economic system, and the United States imposed economic sanctions against Cuba and broke diplomatic relations. An ERS report on the agricultural and food situation in early postrevolutionary Cuba (Mears, 1962) describes how Cuba switched from a market-based relationship with its agricultural trading partners, primarily the United States, to barter arrangements with the Soviet Union, China, and other countries in the East Bloc. As a result, U.S.-Cuba agricultural trade dropped sharply in 1960 and then disappeared almost completely by the middle of 1961.

Table 1. U.S. agricultural exports to Cuba, 1956-58 versus 2012-14

Commodity	Value Annual average		Change	Volume Annual average		Change	Unit value for period		Change
	1956-58	2012-14		1956-58	2012-14		1956-58	2012-14	
	U.S. dollars (millions)		*Percent*	*Metric tons (thousands)*		*Percent*	*U.S. dollars per kilogram*		*Percent*
Total agricultural exports to Cuba	139.17	365.26	162	--	--	--	--	--	--
Animals and products	40.60	161.19	297	119.93	148.18	24	0.34	1.09	221
Chickens, fresh or frozen	0.16	131.00	82,637	0.16	143.09	88,015	0.98	0.92	-6
Pork	9.96	4.33	-56	14.43	1.66	-88	0.69	2.60	278
Lard	21.66	0.02	-100	78.04	0.02	-100	0.28	1.41	409
Tallow	2.74	0.00	-100	15.62	0.00	-100	0.18	--	--
Other	6.09	25.84	324	11.68	3.41	-71	0.52	7.57	1,351
Oilseeds and products	4.81	103.58	2,052	40.07	192.48	380	0.12	0.54	348
Soybean meal	1.46	59.37	3,971	30.67	112.72	268	0.05	0.53	1,008
Soybeans	0.00	44.08	--	0.00	79.71	--	--	0.55	--
Soybean oil	1.69	0.00	-100	5.02	0.00	-100	0.34	--	--
Other oilseeds and products	3.36	0.13	-96	4.38	0.05	-99	0.77	2.77	261
Grains and feeds	53.85	97.26	81	353.63	344.06	-3	0.15	0.28	86
Corn	0.00	72.87	--	0.00	269.20	--	--	0.27	--
Brewing or distilling dregs or waste	0.00	14.06	--	0.00	54.91	--	--	0.26	--
Feeds and fodder, NESOI	0.88	10.30	1,065	--	19.91	--	--	0.52	--
Rice	32.90	0.00	-100	165.56	0.01	-100	0.20	0.67	--
Wheat	5.74	0.00	-100	84.00	0.00	-100	0.07	--	--
Wheat flour	8.27	0.00	-100	79.68	0.00	-100	0.10	--	--
Other grains and feeds	6.05	0.03	-100	24.40	0.03	-100	0.25	0.84	238
Vegetables and preparations	15.77	0.09	-99	105.36	--	--	0.15	--	--
Dried beans	6.44	0.00	-100	39.15	0.00	-100	0.16	--	--
Onions	2.11	0.00	-100	26.88	0.00	-100	0.08	--	--

Commodity	Value Annual average 1956-58	Value Annual average 2012-14	Change	Volume Annual average 1956-58	Volume Annual average 2012-14	Change	Unit value for period 1956-58	Unit value for period 2012-14	Change
	U.S. dollars (millions)		*Percent*	*Metric tons (thousands)*		*Percent*	*U.S. dollars per kilogram*		*Percent*
Other vegetables and preparations	9.34	0.09	-99	66.21	--	--	0.14	--	--
Cotton, excluding linters	3.59	1.04	-71	4.77	0.43	-91	0.75	2.44	224
Fruits and preparations	6.75	0.97	-86	16.33	0.51	-97	0.41	1.90	361
Fruit juices	2.19	0.02	-99	--	--	--	--	--	--
Other agricultural exports to Cuba	13.80	1.12	-92	--	--	--	--	--	--

Notes: Data for 1956-58 are for fiscal years; data for 2012-14 are for calendar years. NESOI = not elsewhere specified or indicated.
Sources: USDA/FAS (1957, 1958, 1959, 2015c).

Table 2. U.S. agricultural imports from Cuba, 1956-58

Commodity	Annual average		Unit value for period
	Value	Volume	
	U.S. dollars (millions)	Metric tons (thousands)	U.S. dollars per kilogram
Total agricultural imports from Cuba	407.50	3,924.46	0.10
Sugar and related products	359.25	3,841.67	0.09
Sugar, cane	333.83	2,844.44	0.12
Molasses	25.43	997.23	0.03
Tobacco, unmanufactured	24.73	10.91	2.27
Coffee	9.55	9.28	1.03
Fruits and preparations	6.05	15.88	0.38
Pineapples, canned or preserved	3.57	12.61	0.28
Pineapples, fresh	1.90	--	--
Other fruits and preparations	0.58	3.27	0.18
Vegetables and preparations	2.62	30.14	0.09
Other agricultural imports from Cuba	5.29	16.59	0.32

Notes: Data are for fiscal years.
Sources: USDA/FAS (1957, 1958, 1959).

The Mears report also describes some of the agricultural trade measures taken by the United States during this period. In July 1960, the United States canceled the remainder of Cuba's sugar quota for 1960 and set the quotas for 1961 and 1962 at zero. Exceptions for U.S. sales of unsubsidized agricultural products and medicine, however, were incorporated within both the partial economic embargo imposed in October 1960 and the much more extensive embargo announced in February 1962, which prohibited all U.S. imports from Cuba.[6]

It was not until May 1964 that the U.S. Department of Commerce revoked the general license for U.S. sales of food and medicine to Cuba and adopted a policy in which licenses for commercial agricultural sales were denied. Only humanitarian donations of agricultural products were approved (Krinsky and Golove, 1993: 114, as cited by Hufbauer et al., 2011: 2-3). Despite efforts by several U.S. administrations to improve U.S.-Cuba relations, the ban on direct agricultural trade with Cuba remained in place for nearly four decades.

Restrictions on indirect trade with Cuba—including agricultural sales by foreign subsidiaries of U.S. companies—have varied over the years. In October 1975, the U.S. Department of Treasury revoked the regulation that prohibited such subsidiaries from trading with Cuba and instead began to require licenses for such transactions (Franklin, 1997: 119-121, as cited by USITC, 2001: 2-5 to 2-6). With the passage of the Cuban Democracy Act in October 1992, however, the Treasury Department lost the authority to issue these licenses for most trade with Cuba (Ross, 2004). Prior to the law, licensed agricultural sales to Cuba by foreign subsidiaries of U.S. firms were in the neighborhood of $350 million per year (Fletcher, 1992, as cited by Wong, 1994).

U.S. Agricultural Exports to Cuba Resume

The current state of U.S.-Cuba agricultural trade is founded upon a major policy change implemented about 15 years ago. In October 2000, the Trade Sanctions Reform and Export Enhancement Act (TSRA)—which authorized certain sales of food, medicines, and medical equipment to a number of countries, including Cuba—was signed into law. At that time, nearly a decade had passed since the dissolution of the Soviet Union and the concomitant end to Soviet economic support for Cuba. In this context, the Cuban Government overcame its initial reluctance to import basic agricultural commodities from the United States in order to supplement domestic production and, when necessary, to respond to short-term food shortages caused by adverse weather conditions. The devastation caused by Hurricane Michelle in November 2001 was an especially strong factor behind the change in Cuba's stance toward importing U.S. agricultural products (Messina, 2015).

TSRA's exemptions to the embargo quickly led to the reestablishment of U.S. agricultural exports to Cuba (fig. 1). However, TSRA does not include a legal framework for the resumption of U.S. agricultural imports from Cuba. From 1960 through the mid-1990s, the U.S. economic embargo on Cuba was largely authorized by Executive Orders. This changed with the passage of the Cuban Liberty and Democratic Solidarity Act of 1996 (also known as the Helms-Burton Act, in reference to the law's sponsors, Senator Jesse Helms of North Carolina and Representative Dan Burton of Indiana). The Helms-Burton Act codifies the embargo (in other words, requires the embargo by law) and defines the conditions for suspending and then terminating the embargo. Specifically, the Act authorizes the President to suspend the embargo when a transition government comes to power in Cuba and to end the embargo altogether when a democratically elected government takes power there.[7] In the absence of new legislation that modifies these provisions, U.S. agricultural imports from Cuba remain at zero, even though Cuba still produces many of the agricultural commodities that it formerly exported to the United States, such as sugar and tobacco.

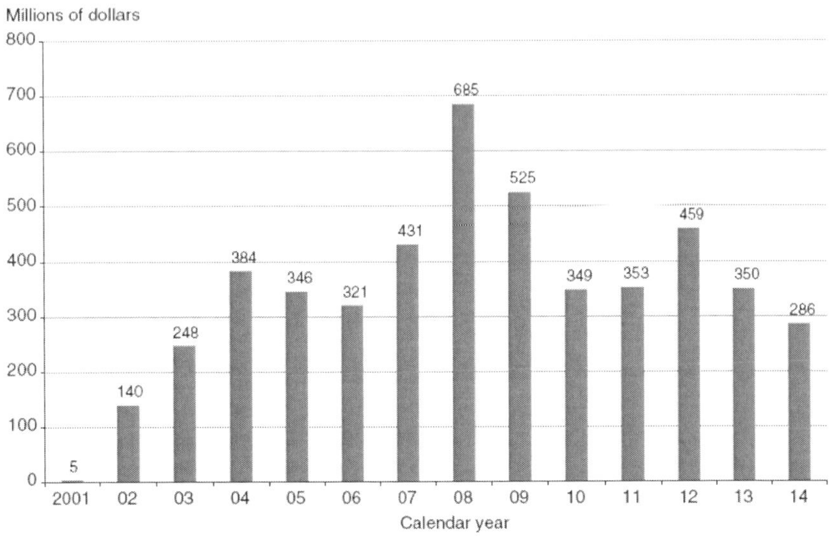

Source: USDA/FAS (2015a).

Figure 1. U.S. agricultural exports to Cuba averaged $365 million per year during 2012-14 Millions of dollars.

Foreign Agricultural Sales to Cuba

U.S. agricultural exports to Cuba averaged $365 million per year during 2012-14. Exports are heavily concentrated in four basic commodities (table 1). Chicken meat, corn, soybean meal, and soybeans accounted for 84 percent of total exports during this period in terms of value. Cuba is an important market for U.S. broiler meat (Davis et al., 2013). On a quantity basis, Cuba ranked as the fourth largest export market for U.S. broiler meat during 2012-14. Frozen chicken-leg quarters, a relatively low-cost poultry cut, accounted for 83 percent of U.S. broiler meat exports to Cuba in terms of quantity during this period. Corn, soybean meal, and soybeans are all feedstuffs used in livestock production in Cuba. In some years during the TSRA period, U.S. agricultural exports to Cuba have included substantial quantities of commodities other than the four mentioned above, such as rice, wheat, nonfat dry milk, pork, dried beans, and soybean oil.[8] U.S. restrictions on extending credit to Cuban buyers have made it harder for U.S. agricultural exporters to sell a larger volume and broader variety of commodities to Cuba.

The United States is not Cuba's only foreign supplier of agricultural products. Export data reported by Cuba's trading partners indicate that Cuba's agricultural imports from all countries averaged $1.8 billion per year during 2012-14 (fig. 2). The United States was Cuba's second leading supplier of agricultural imports during this period ($362 million), while the European Union (EU) ($383 million) and Brazil ($348 million) were Cuba's first and third leading suppliers. Together, these three trade partners supplied 61 percent of Cuba's agricultural imports, with the U.S. share equaling 20 percent. From 2003 to 2012, the United States was Cuba's leading supplier of agricultural imports. The United States slipped to second in 2013 and third in 2014.

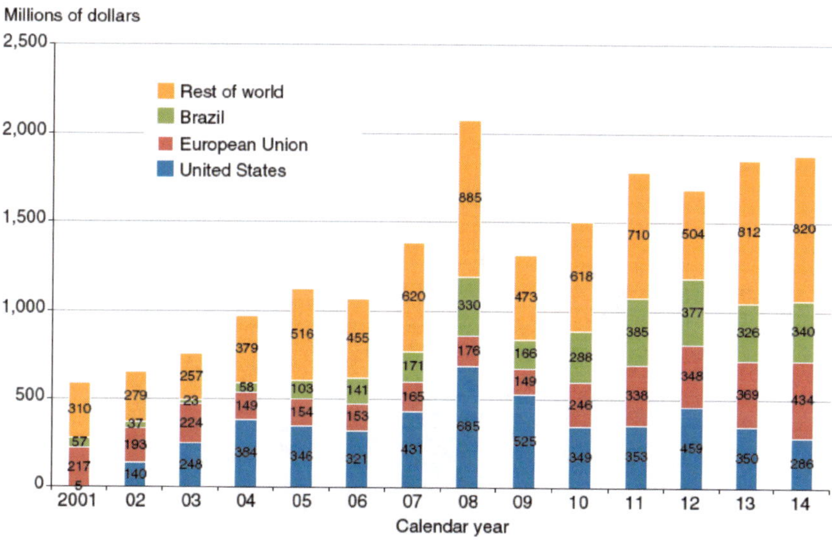

Sources: USDA/FAS (2015a) and export data of various national governments, as cited by Global Trade Information Services (2015).

Figure 2. Cuba's agricultural imports have trended upward over the past decade Millions of dollars.

Cuba's total agricultural imports have been trending upward over the past decade, increasing by 94 percent between 2004 and 2014. The value of these imports was unusually large ($2.1 billion) in 2008, due in part to high commodity prices. In fact, the unit values of each of the top five U.S.

agricultural exports to Cuba (fresh or frozen chicken, corn, wheat, soybeans, and soybean meal) increased by at least 67 percent between 2006 and 2008. Hurricane Ike also contributed to the large value of imports in 2008, as U.S. agricultural exports to Cuba in October and November of that year were larger than the corresponding months in any other year during 2001-14. Cuba's agricultural imports are concentrated in grains and animal products (fig. 3). During 2012-14, the five leading agricultural imports in terms of value were wheat (13 percent), corn (12 percent), chicken meat (11 percent), nonfat dried milk (10 percent), and rice (10 percent).

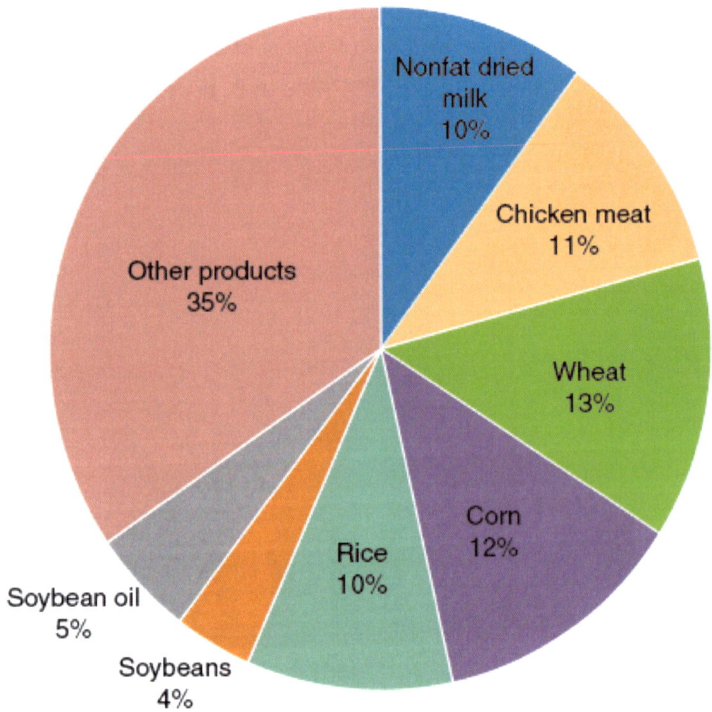

Source: Export data of various national governments, as cited by Global Trade Information Services (2015).

Figure 3. Cuba's agricultural imports from the world were concentrated in grains and animal products from 2012 to 2014.

U.S. Agricultural Exports Limited by Payment Requirements and Financial Restrictions

A major inhibitor of U.S. agricultural exports to Cuba is the TSRA's restrictions on the terms of payment and financing. TSRA specifies that the only payment or financing terms that U.S. persons may provide for U.S. agricultural exports to Cuba are (1) payment of cash in advance or (2) financing by third-country financial institutions. Moreover, TSRA underscores that nothing in its specification of payment and financing restrictions "authorizes payment terms or trade financing involving a debit or credit to an account of a person located in Cuba or of the Government of Cuba maintained on the books of a United States depository institution" (U.S. Statutes at Large, 2000). Many observers believe that this credit restriction enables other countries to compete more effectively with the United States for agricultural sales to Cuba, as exporters in those countries are able to leverage their sales to Cuba by extending credit and favorable payment terms, while U.S. exporters are prohibited from doing so (Messina, 2015; U.S. International Trade Commission (USITC), 2007).

A ruling issued in 2005 clarifies TSRA's restrictions on cash-in-advance payments. From the implementation of TSRA in 2000 until late 2004, U.S. exporters of agricultural products to Cuba generally believed that it was possible to comply with TSRA's cash-in-advance option by authorizing the transfer of the documents necessary for transferring ownership of the goods to the Cuban importer just after receiving the cash payment. This meant that the cash payment would not be in place until sometime after the shipment had left the U.S. port. In late 2004, however, a number of U.S. financial institutions started to block such transactions due to their uncertain conformity with TSRA's conditions for cash-in-advance payments.

In February 2005, the U.S. Department of the Treasury's Office of Foreign Assets Control issued a ruling that payment of cash in advance means that the payment must be received by the seller or the seller's agent prior to shipment of goods from the U.S. port at which they are loaded. Following this ruling, Cuba began to make payments for its purchases of U.S. agricultural products by using "a confirmed, irrevocable letter-of-credit ... completed with a third country bank" (USDA, Foreign Agricultural Service, Office of Global Analysis, 2008: 24). This change was reportedly motivated by concerns that the new ruling might allow agricultural shipments destined for Cuba to be confiscated in U.S. ports in conjunction with any outstanding legal claims against the Cuban Government (USITC, 2007: 3-5 to 3-6).

Financing by a third-country financial institution is more laborious than making a conventional payment directly from the buyer's financial institution in Cuba to the seller's financial institution in the United States.[9] The Cuban Government adjusted to this technique when buying U.S. agricultural products, although some U.S. agricultural commodity groups viewed the requirement of using third-country financial institutions as an important obstacle.[10] By contrast, the U.S. prohibition on extending credit to Cuba's agricultural importers continues to hamper U.S. efforts to export agricultural products to Cuba. During 2005-07, the United States exported an annual average of 124,000 metric tons of rice, 275,000 metric tons of wheat, 6,000 metric tons of nonfat dried milk, and 33,000 metric tons of soybean oil to Cuba. During 2012-14, however, the United States exported hardly any rice, wheat, nonfat dried milk, or soybean oil to Cuba, even though Cuba purchased an annual average of 110,000 metric tons of rice and 75,000 metric tons of soybean oil from Brazil, 462,000 metric tons of wheat from France, and 10,000 metric tons of whole milk powder from New Zealand (Global Trade Information Services, 2015).

Factors other than financial restrictions and payment requirements influence the level of U.S. agricultural exports to Cuba. For instance, the United States consistently exported small quantities of frozen pork muscle cuts and pork variety meats to Cuba over the past decade, except in 2014 when a number of factors made those products more expensive to potential buyers in Cuba. U.S. pork prices were high due to short supplies caused by the porcine epidemic diarrhea virus, and the U.S. dollar was particularly strong. As a result, Cuba imported no muscle cuts of pork from the United States and a smaller volume of pork variety meats in 2014. In addition, Coleman (2009: 6) suggests that Cuba's choice of agricultural importers is the product of noncommercial factors, such as the Cuban Government's desire to have a diverse set of import suppliers, to strengthen its geopolitical relationships with allies such as China and Vietnam, and to curry favor in specific U.S. States or Congressional Districts on the topic of U.S.-Cuba economic relations.

Cuba Is an Established Exporter of Sugar But Few Other Agricultural Products

Import data reported by Cuba's trading partners indicate that Cuba's total agricultural exports (to all countries) averaged $526 million per year during 2012-14 (fig. 4). The leading destinations for these exports were China (including Hong Kong), accounting for 45 percent of the total, and the EU, accounting for 36 percent. Some of these exports are not the result of stand-alone commercial transactions but are linked instead to broader trade and foreign investment deals. For instance, Cuba has an agreement to sell China about 400,000 metric tons of sugar each year, while China has extended loans to Cuba and made direct investments in Cuban oil exploration, petroleum refining, port development, and tourism (Frank, 2013; Rey Mallén, 2014; Menéndez, 2015). By contrast, Cuba's agricultural exports to the EU—which include such commodities as sugar, tobacco, and natural honey—suggest a commercial relationship akin to that between the EU and other Caribbean countries. Cuba received preferential access to the EU market through the EU's General System of Preferences (GSP) until 2013, when Cuba was recognized in United Nations statistics as an upper middle-income country (European Union Delegation to Cuba, 2015).

Russia is currently the third leading destination for Cuba's agricultural exports, although Cuba's agricultural exports to Russia are not much larger in value than its exports to Sweden or Belarus. Russia accounted for 5 percent of Cuba's total agricultural exports during 2012-14. During the Cold War, the Soviet Union heavily subsidized the Cuban economy by importing sugar at well above the world market price (Messina, 2015), and as recently as 2001, Cuban agricultural exports to Russia equaled $420 million, compared with $51 million in 2014. A disagreement during the early 2000s regarding the repayment of loans and obligations owed to Russia appears to have soured the Cuba-Russia economic relationship, although reports last year suggest that this relationship is on the mend (Tamayo, 2014).

Sugar accounts for the overwhelming majority of Cuba's agricultural exports to the world. During 2012-14, Cuba's sugar exports averaged $470 million per year, accounting for 89 percent of the country's total agricultural exports. Natural honey, with exports averaging $19 million per year (3 percent of the total), was Cuba's second leading agricultural export. Among Cuba's nonagricultural exports are several products that are manufactured using the agricultural commodities of either tobacco or sugarcane. Cuba has long been known for its cigars. During 2012-14, cigar and cigarette exports averaged $222 million per year. These exports increased substantially during the first several years of the 21st century and have fluctuated since then. In addition, Cuba has reestablished itself as an important exporter of rum and tafia, with export value growing from $27 million in 2005 to $91 million in 2014.[11]

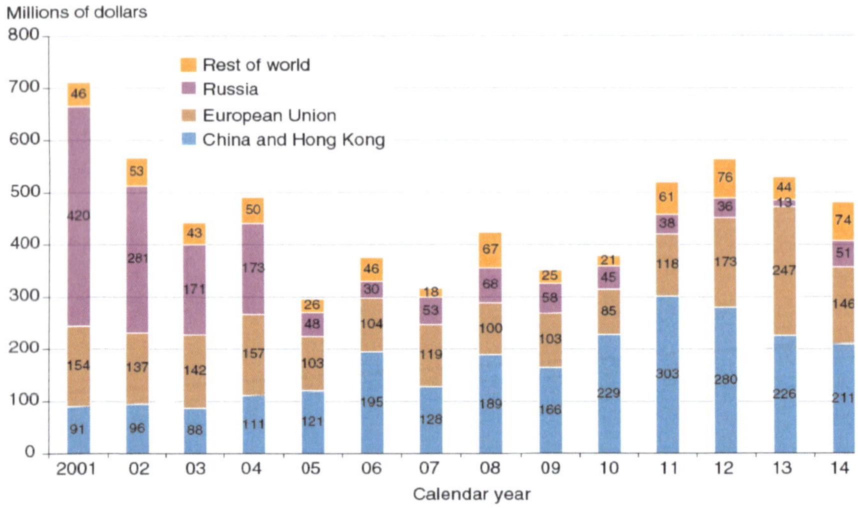

Sources: USDA/FAS (2015a), and import data of various national governments, as cited by Global Trade Information Services (2015).

Figure 4. China and the European Union are the leading destinations for Cuba's agricultural exports.

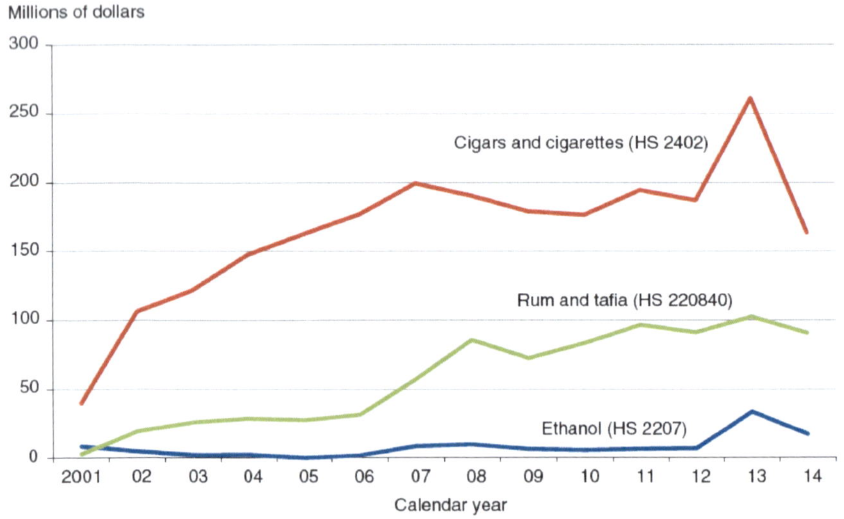

Source: Import data of various national governments, as cited by Global Trade Information Services (2015).

Figure 5. Cuba's exports of ethanol, cigars, rum, and tafia grew substantially over the past decade.

The Cuban Rice Sector

Cuba's diversification away from U.S. rice imports represents the loss of a lucrative export opportunity for U.S. rice growers, since Cuba has the highest per capita rice consumption of any country in the Western Hemisphere. Annual per capita rice supply (milled equivalent) is about 61 kilograms in Cuba, 49 kilograms in Costa Rica and the Dominican Republic, 44 kilograms in Nicaragua, and 7 kilograms in the United States, according to Food Balance Sheets for 2011-13 from the Food and Agriculture Organization of the United Nations (2015). Today, Cuba imports about half of its annual rice consumption, with rice imports averaging about 435,000 tons per year during 2010-14. Vietnam supplies 70 percent or more of Cuba's rice imports—mostly 5 and 15 percent broken long-grain milled rice—while Brazil supplies most of the remainder. Brazil has been a major supplier of rice to Cuba since 2012.

In 2013/14, Cuba produced 423,000 tons of rice (milled basis), nearly unchanged from the previous year but up 18 percent from 2000/01 (USDA/FAS, 2015c). Rice area, yield, and production in Cuba can vary by a wide margin each year due to weather and input availability. Cuba plants two rice crops a year. The main crop is planted in April-July and harvested in August-December. The second crop is planted in December-February and harvested in March-June. Crop calendars, of course, vary somewhat across producers, regions, and time. The largest producing Provinces are Pinar del Rio, Granma, and Sancti Spiritus. Some producers are able to harvest a second partial or "ratoon" crop from the stubble of the first crop harvest.

Cooperative farms, producers with use privileges on state-owned land, and small-scale farmers account for the bulk of the area devoted to rice in Cuba, according to official Cuban data for 2009 (República de Cuba, Oficina Nacional de Estadística, 2010). Since 2009/10, rice area has averaged 203,000 hectares per year, up from an average of 144,000 hectares during the previous 5 years. The Cuban Government wants to boost domestic rice production and reduce imports, especially after the 2007/08 price spike and export bans by some rice-exporting countries, and has received technical assistance dedicated to the rice sector from several rice-producing countries, including Brazil, Japan, and Vietnam.

Cuba's field yields averaged 2.8 metric tons per hectare (rough-rice basis) from 2009/10 to 2013/14 and have shown no signs of long-term growth since the late 1970s. Cuba's yields are low compared with other rice growing countries in the region. From 2009/10 to 2013/14, rice yields averaged 4.7 metric tons per hectare in the Dominican Republic, 4.4 metric tons in

Nicaragua, and 3.5 metric tons in Costa Rica. Traditionally, researchers have pointed to a lack of inputs (chemicals, fertilizers, and irrigation infrastructure) and the continued participation of state farms in rice production as the main factors explaining Cuba's lower yields (Alvarez, 2004).

The Cuban Sugar Sector

Cuba's sugar industry is much smaller than it was during the Cold War (fig. 6). At its peak, Cuba produced between 6.5 million and 8.5 million metric tons of sugar annually, with over 90 percent of production destined for export, on average. If Cuba's current production and export levels equaled those of the 1980s (marketing years 1981/82 to 1990/91), Cuba would be the world's 7th largest producer and 3rd largest exporter of sugar (table 3). The Soviet Union was Cuba's leading customer for sugar during the 1980s; following the Soviet Union's dissolution in 1991, there was a precipitous decline in Cuban sugar production and exports. For marketing years 2012/13 to 2014/15, Cuba's sugar production and exports are estimated to have averaged about 1.6 million metric tons and 967,000 metric tons per year, respectively.

Foreign investment from Brazil has helped Cuba to increase its sugar production over the past several years (Messina, 2015). In 2012, a Brazilian firm signed a 13-year agreement to manage a Cuban sugar mill jointly with Grupo Azucarero (AZCUBA), Cuba's state-owned industrial group in the sugar sector, and a British firm signed an agreement to produce biogas using sugarcane bagasse and other feedstocks (Grogg, 2013; Birch, 2015). Despite the increased emphasis on producing distilled spirits and bioenergy from Cuban sugarcane, exports continue to be important for the sector. During 2012-14, exports accounted for about 52 percent of Cuban sugar production (calculated using data in table 3). Russia remained Cuba's largest export market for sugar through 2004 (fig. 7). Since then, China has been Cuba's largest export market. Given its contract to supply China with 400,000 metric tons of sugar each year, Cuba's annual sugar exports to China have ranged from about 370,000 to 438,000 metric tons over the past decade (2005-14), according to Chinese import data cited by Global Trade Information Services (2015). Cuba also has offset some of its lost sugar exports to Russia by increasing sales to the EU.

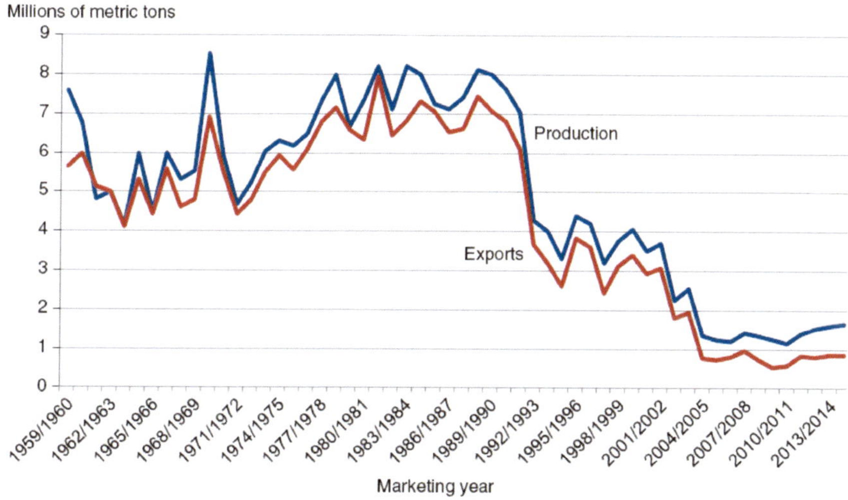

Source: USDA/FAS (2015b).

Figure 6. Cuba's role as a sugar producer and exporter greatly diminished after the Soviet Union's dissolution in 1991.

Table 3. World sugar production and exports: Averages, marketing years 2012/13 to 2014/15

Country	Production *Thousands of metric tons*	Country	Exports *Thousands of metric tons*
Brazil	37,417	Brazil	26,133
India	27,808	Thailand	7,298
European Union	16,475	**Cuba, 1981/82 to 1990/91**	**7,003**
China	13,088	Australia	3,301
Thailand	10,776	Mexico	2,116
United States	7,853	Guatemala	2,070
Cuba, 1981/82 to 1990/91	**7,706**	India	1,755
Mexico	6,712	European Union	1,571
Pakistan	5,287	**Cuba, 2012/13 to 2014/15**	**967**
Russia	4,583	Pakistan	810
Australia	4,443	Colombia	717

Table 3. (Continued)

Country	Production *Thousands of metric tons*	Country	Exports *Thousands of metric tons*
Guatemala	2,847	South Africa	656
Philippines	2,467	United Arab Emirates	624
Indonesia	2,233	Algeria	500
Colombia	2,200	Belarus	489
South Africa	2,190	El Salvador	438
Turkey	2,162	Mauritius	431
Argentina	2,077	Nicaragua	393
Egypt	2,027	Swaziland	371
Ukraine	1,910	Egypt	367
Vietnam	1,667	South Korea	353
Cuba, 2012/13 to 2014/15	**1,592**	Malaysia	310
Iran	1,340	Philippines	275
Peru	1,150	Azerbaijan	248
Japan	750	United States	236

Note: Data include both cane and beet sugar.
Source: USDA/FAS (2015b).

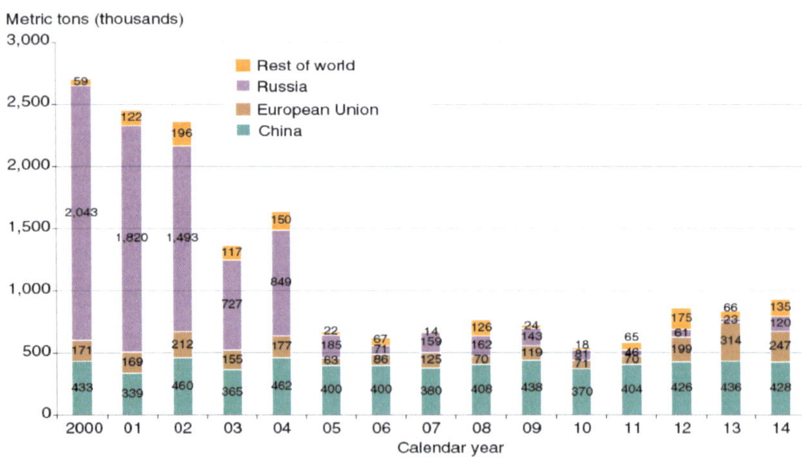

Source: Import data of national governments, as cited by Global Trade Information.

Figure 7. Cuba's sugar exports by destination, 2000-2014.

U.S.-CUBA POSSIBLE FUTURE

Two countries enjoy normal trade relations (NTR), formerly referred to as most-favored-nation (MFN) status, when each country provides to the other the same trade benefits that it provides to any other country with which it has NTR. For agricultural trade, this includes the application of MFN tariffs to any imports originating in the other country. In addition, countries that have established NTR with each other generally do not prohibit routine, short-term travel from one country to the other for the purposes of business or pleasure. The executive actions announced in December 2014 are a small step toward NTR between Cuba and the United States. While the executive actions modify the payment and financial restrictions governing U.S. exports to Cuba and provide for additional exemptions to the U.S. economic embargo, they provide no opportunities for U.S. agricultural imports from Cuba, save for the small purchases that licensed travelers to Cuba are allowed to bring home. Given the terms of the Helms-Burton Act, congressional action is required—in the absence of a democratically elected government in Cuba—to make more substantial changes to the economic embargo.

Establishment of NTR with Cuba is likely to have both short-term and long-term effects on U.S.- Cuba agricultural trade. The short-term effects would be from the immediate removal of certain restrictions—say, the ban on U.S. agricultural imports from Cuba—while the long-term effects would be from the additional economic growth and reduced transaction costs stimulated by the policy changes. Of particular importance to agricultural trade are sectors in the Cuban economy that rely on intermediate and final agricultural imports—such as tourism, restaurants, food services, livestock production, and food manufacturing—and sectors in which Cuba specializes due to its resource endowments and acquired comparative advantages, such as fruit, vegetables, sugar, and tobacco. (For sugar, access to the U.S. market depends on U.S. sugar policy.)

Even the short-term effects of establishing NTR with Cuba are potentially large for U.S. agricultural exports. Partial-equilibrium models (USITC, 2007) suggest that if all U.S. financing and travel restrictions had been eliminated in 2006, U.S. agricultural exports to Cuba would have increased from $321 million to roughly $550 million. However, the authors of the USITC study caution against summing the partial-equilibrium results for each commodity to obtain the total effect of removing restrictions, since their models do not take into account cross-commodity substitutions. A separate analysis by Rosson, et al. (2010) using an input/output model indicates that U.S. exports to Cuba would increase by up to $365 million per year if U.S. financing and travel restrictions were removed, including some $327 million in additional agricultural exports, as defined by USDA.

The Updated U.S. Approach to Cuba

The new U.S. approach to Cuba contains several key elements that have the potential to affect U.S.- Cuba agricultural trade, albeit in small ways.[12] Several of these elements are intended to remove outright obstacles to bilateral trade, others are designed to reduce transaction costs, and still others aim at fostering greater growth in the Cuban economy. The first element is the effort to ***reestablish diplomatic relations with Cuba***. In January 2015, a U.S. delegation met with Cuban officials in Havana to discuss a wide range of issues, and several subsequent rounds of meetings have been held (Whitefield, 2015). While these efforts alone do not ensure increased agricultural trade between the two countries, they portend a more favorable economic and policy environment for bilateral agricultural trade over the medium and long term.

The second element is the ***relaxation of some U.S. restrictions on travelling to Cuba***. Specifically, the U.S. Government is expanding the set of classifications of U.S. citizens and permanent residents who may visit Cuba under general license from the U.S. Government, requiring no special approval. The added classifications are:

- Public performances, clinics, workshops, athletic and other competitions, and exhibitions;
- Support for the Cuban people;
- Humanitarian projects;
- Activities of private foundations or research and educational institutes;
- Exportation, importation, or transmission of information or information materials; and
- Certain export transactions that may be considered for authorization under existing regulations and guidelines.[13]

This loosening of travel restrictions could have a small, positive impact on U.S. agricultural exports to Cuba by making it easier for people pursuing authorized export transactions to travel there. However, other export restrictions that are still in place, most notably the limitations on financing and credit, are likely more onerous than the previous set of travel restrictions. Increased travel involving private foundations, research or educational institutions, and the dissemination of information might not immediately result in more U.S. agricultural sales to Cuba, but could strengthen Cuban ties with the U.S. agribusiness and academic sectors, which could help the further development of production agriculture in Cuba.

The third element consists of ***additional exemptions to the embargo on U.S. exports to Cuba***. New items authorized for export include certain building materials for private residential construction, goods for use by entrepreneurs in the Cuban private sector, and tools and equipment for private-sector agricultural activity. These new exemptions could also stimulate additional agricultural trade between Cuba and the United States. For instance, small-scale Cuban poultry producers who import farm equipment may increase their feedstuff imports from the United States (and other countries). In addition, licensed U.S. travelers to Cuba will be allowed to import up to $400 worth of goods for personal use, with a limit of $100 for tobacco and alcohol combined. This policy change is likely to result in the resumption of U.S. agricultural imports from Cuba, albeit on a small scale, to the extent that any agricultural products are among the goods allowed.

The fourth element is the further ***relaxation of U.S. restrictions on remittances to Cuba***. Remittances are transfers of money sent by a migrant or immigrant to people in his or her country of origin.[14] Since 2009, the United States has placed no limits on the amount of money one can remit to close relatives in Cuba. The new policy approach will raise the limit on general donative remittances to Cuban nationals (except to certain officials of the government or the Communist Party) from $500 to $2,000 per quarter. Moreover, specific licenses will no longer be required for donative remittances for humanitarian projects, support for the Cuban people, and support for the development of private businesses in Cuba—nor for remittances from remittance forwarding services other than financial institutions.

Increased remittances to Cuba could increase consumer budgets, thereby enabling additional foreign agricultural sales to Cuba. Also, some remittances could be used to invest in agricultural production or retail establishments. Regression analysis by Romanò and Echevarría León (2015) indicates that remittances are a significant determinant of whether a Cuban worker in Havana will pursue legal self-employment ("cuentapropismo"). While the higher ceiling on remittances could allow for a quadrupling of U.S. remittances to Cuba (to people who are not close relatives), the extent to which the previous set of restrictions was a binding constraint will not be apparent until future levels of remittances are recorded. Already, U.S. remittances to Cuba are quite large—in the neighborhood of $1.4 billion to $2.5 billion per year (U.S. Department of State, Bureau of Western Hemisphere Affairs, 2013; Kandell, 2015).

The fifth element is a set of ***policy changes intended to facilitate authorized transactions*** between the United States and Cuba. The regulatory definition of the statutory term "cash in advance" was revised to specify that it means "cash before transfer of title." This regulatory change addresses the concern that the revised definition of the term issued in February 2005 adversely affected U.S. agricultural exports to Cuba. The U.S. Department of Treasury's interpretation in 2005 required that cash payments be made before the goods left a U.S. port, whereas the revised interpretation is more reflective of normal cash-in-advance arrangements.[15] In addition, U.S. institutions will now be permitted to open correspondent accounts at Cuban financial institutions to facilitate the processing of authorized transactions, and U.S. credit and debit cards will be permitted for use by travelers to Cuba. These changes will lower the transaction costs for U.S. exports to Cuba by reducing the liquidity constraint of the payment method and opening new avenues for cash flows, thereby increasing the opportunities for trade. However, the policy changes still do not allow U.S. exporters to extend credit to their Cuban buyers, which places U.S. agricultural exporters at a competitive disadvantage with other exporting countries. By contrast, South Korea's state-run Korea Trade Insurance Corporation signed a memorandum of understanding in February 2015 for a credit line worth $67.9 million in order to facilitate Korean exports to Cuba (Yonhap News Agency, 2015).

The sixth element concerns the intention of the U.S. Government to assist with ***providing internet access to a greater share of the Cuban population***. The commercial export of certain consumer communications devices, related software, applications, hardware, services, and items for the establishment and update of communications-related systems will be permitted. Telecommunications providers will be allowed to establish the necessary mechanisms, including infrastructure, in Cuba to provide commercial telecommunications and internet services. These changes are intended to improve telecommunications between Cuba and the rest of the world, which may also facilitate U.S.-Cuba trade. In addition, wireless telecommunications in the developing world is key to helping buyers and sellers of agricultural products to find better prices.

Finally, the seventh element ***updates the application of U.S. sanctions on Cuba in third countries***. U.S.-owned or -controlled entities in third countries will be generally licensed to provide services to, and engage in financial transactions with, Cuban individuals in third countries. In addition, general licenses will unblock the accounts at U.S. banks of Cuban nationals who have relocated outside of Cuba, permit U.S. persons to participate in third-country professional meetings and conferences related to Cuba, and allow foreign vessels to enter the United States after engaging in certain humanitarian trade with Cuba, among other measures. The end of these restrictions may have unknown but positive implications for U.S.-Cuba agricultural trade.

Might a "Normal" Agricultural Trading Relationship with Cuba Look Like the Dominican Republic?

For U.S. exports, a more normal agricultural trading relationship between the United States and Cuba might resemble the current relationship between the United States and the Dominican Republic. As large countries in the Caribbean, Cuba and the Dominican Republic are similar in many ways. The populations are similar (11.1 million for Cuba versus 10.5 million for the Dominican Republic, according to estimates for 2015 from the U.S. Department of Commerce, Bureau of the Census (2013)), as is per capita income (about $10,200 for Cuba in 2010 and $12,800 for the Dominican Republic in 2014 in terms of purchasing power parity, according to estimates by the Central Intelligence Agency (2015)).[16]

As destinations for U.S. agricultural exports, however, Cuba and the Dominican Republic differ in several respects. During 2012-14, U.S. agricultural exports to the Dominican Republic ($1.1 billion, annual average) were more than triple the size of exports to Cuba ($365 million) (table 4). Also, U.S. agricultural exports to the Dominican Republic cover a wider range of commodities than exports to Cuba (table 4). Thus, a more normal agricultural trading relationship between the United States and Cuba might feature a much larger level of U.S. agricultural exports to Cuba, including commodities that the United States sold to Cuba during the 2000s but not recently—such as dry milk, wheat, rice, and dried beans—and perhaps even intermediate and consumer-oriented commodities that Cuba has never imported from the United States in large quantities.

Table 4. U.S. agricultural exports to the Dominican Republic and Cuba: Annual averages, 2012-14

Product	Exports to the Dominican Republic		Exports to Cuba	
	Value	Volume	Value	Volume
	Dollars (thousands)	*Metric tons (thousands)*	*Dollars (thousands)*	*Metric tons (thousands)*
Total agricultural exports	1,149.643	--	365.255	--
Animals and animal products	233.699	--	161.192	--
Beef and veal	40.351	4.584	0.041	0.042
Pork	40.700	16.363	4.331	1.663
Chicken meat, fresh or frozen	21.156	18.204	148.925	143.085
Turkey meat, fresh or frozen	10.840	4.807	1.112	0.722
Nonfat dry milk	28.131	7.779	0	0
Cheese	19.961	4.318	0	0
Other animals and animal products	72.560	--	6.783	--
Grains and feeds	331.272	852.667	97.257	344.061
Wheat, unmilled	158.847	494.020	0	0
Corn	67.430	303.728	72.869	269.198
Prepared foods obtained by the swelling or roasting of cereals or cereal products, not containing sugar	35.828	6.155	0	0
Brewing or distilling dregs or waste	0.271	1.074	14.055	54.912
Mixed feeds, not elsewhere specified or indicated	1.469	1.283	10.279	19.914
Other grains and feeds	67.427	46.407	0.054	0.037
Fruit and preparations	34.322	22.522	0.973	0.511

Product	Exports to the Dominican Republic		Exports to Cuba	
	Value	Volume	Value	Volume
	Dollars (thousands)	*Metric tons (thousands)*	*Dollars (thousands)*	*Metric tons (thousands)*
Apples, fresh	15.363	14.363	0.104	0.087
Other fruit and preparations	18.959	8.159	0.869	0.424
Fruit juices[1]	13.029	9.160	0.015	0.006
Vegetables and preparations	46.850	--	0.090	--
Dried beans	24.302	23.853	0	0
Other vegetables and preparations	22.548	--	0.090	--
Oilseeds and products	292.231	458.598	103.584	192.478
Soybean meal	186.780	359.247	59.371	112.721
Soybean oil	64.918	68.958	0	0
Soybeans	0.345	0.624	44.083	79.710
Other oilseeds and products	40.188	--	0.130	--
Tobacco, unmanufactured	89.898	9.027	0	0
Essential oils	10.315	0.920	0	0
Sugar and tropical products	20.337	8.402	0.063	0.009
Other horticultural products	50.553	--	1.029	--
Other agricultural exports	27.137	--	1.052	--

[1]Volume is measured in millions of liters, and unit value is measured in dollars per liter.

Source: USDA/FAS (2015a).

Given the geographic proximity of Cuba and the United States, part of the increase in U.S. agricultural exports to Cuba may come from the diversion of other countries' exports to Cuba. Import data for HS chapters 01, 02, and 04-24 indicate that the U.S. share of the Dominican Republic's agricultural imports was about 45 percent in 2013 (United Nations, Department of Economic and Social Affairs, Statistics Division, 2015). By contrast, the U.S. share of Cuba's agricultural exports was about 20 percent during 2012-14. Expansion of tourist-oriented food services in Cuba could also boost U.S. agricultural sales to Cuba, including such products as cheese, yogurt, and higher value cuts of pork, poultry meat, and beef.

For U.S. imports, Cuba's current agricultural exports to the world might be indicative of the country's initial ability to export agricultural products to the United States. Sugar and tobacco currently account for about 70 percent of Cuba's agricultural exports to the world, but it is not known whether future U.S. sugar policy would allow for significant imports from Cuba. Over time, Cuba is likely to develop comparative advantages in the production and export of certain citrus and tropical fruit (Kost, 2004b, 2004c), vegetables, tropical plants, and cut flowers, although this will require greater investment. Over the past several decades, Cuba is reported to have made strides in organic production, due in part to the decreased availability of pesticides, fertilizers, and petroleum that resulted from the dissolution of the Soviet Union (United Nations Environment Programme, 2015; Zepeda, 2003; Kost, 2004a).

Rice

With establishment of a more normal trading relationship between Cuba and the United States, the U.S. rice industry would be likely again to sell rice to Cuba and may be able to regain a large share of Cuba's import market, but only if U.S. suppliers are able to provide competitive terms of credit. Several factors favor U.S. rice suppliers in the Cuban market. First, the United States is a consistent, year-round supplier of the high-quality rice that is attractive to Cuban consumers. Second, the United States enjoys a distinct transportation advantage over Cuba's current rice suppliers. The Port of New Orleans is about two sailing days away from the Port of Mariel, compared with more than 30 days for the Vietnamese port of Ho Chi Minh City.[17] This transportation advantage partially offsets the higher price of U.S. rice compared with rice from Vietnam. U.S. rice typically sells at a higher price than rice from Asian exporters because of differences in quality. As of late May 2015, U.S. prices were about $130 per metric ton (36 percent) above prices for comparable grades of Vietnamese rice, but about $65 below Brazil's prices. Because the United States is able to ship many smaller-sized cargoes throughout the year to ports throughout Cuba, there is an opportunity for Cuba to reduce the internal trucking costs associated with distributing large shipments of rice arriving in the Port of Mariel to local markets. Third, the United States has the potential to export rough rice to Cuba, which could then be fully milled there. Asia's rice exporting countries generally do not allow exports of rough rice. Brazil currently exports rough rice mostly to Central and South America. Fourth, if Cuba opens up further as a tourist destination, demand for high-quality rice would increase, supporting increased U.S. sales.

Meat and Dairy Products

To the extent that the relaxation of trade and travel restrictions spurs economic growth in Cuba, a more normal trading relationship should stimulate U.S. exports to Cuba of meat and dairy products. Animal proteins are a luxury in Cuba, and exports of significant volumes of high-value meat and dairy products will require further growth in the disposable incomes of Cuban consumers. In the near term, U.S. exports of low-value muscle cuts of pork, pork variety meats, chicken leg quarters, and milk powder are more likely to increase, but this trade growth also will depend on further income growth. Cuban demand for imported pork, for instance, is concentrated in products with a lower unit value, such as pork trim, butts, hams, and pork variety meats. Trim, butts, and hams are typically used as inputs into further processed pork products such as sausage and lunch meats, types of protein that are affordable, convenient, and attractive to consumers in upper middle-income countries such as Cuba. Fewer U.S. restrictions on travelling to Cuba could induce Cuban import demand for higher value meat cuts as the hotel, restaurant, and institutional sectors develop.

Sugar

A more normal trading relationship with Cuba would likely result in the establishment of some U.S. sugar imports from Cuba, but at volumes much smaller than during the late 1950s. The United States is a net importer of sugar, but most of its sugar imports come from Mexico, which has duty-free access as part of the North American Free Trade Agreement (NAFTA).[18] The United States uses a tariff-rate quota (TRQ) system, instituted through the Agreement on Agriculture of the World Trade Organization (WTO), to manage its sugar imports from most other countries. Cuba is a WTO member, so if Cuba were allocated quota space within the TRQ, some level of imports would likely occur, depending on the size of the quota and conditions within the U.S. market.

Boughner and Coleman (2002) discuss six options for normalizing Cuban access to the U.S. sugar market that are compliant with U.S. obligations under its multilateral trade agreements at the World Trade Organization (WTO): (1) allocating quotas on a first-come, first served basis; (2) auctioning the quotas; (3) redistributing the TRQ among countries, including Cuba; (4) increasing the TRQ to accommodate Cuba; (5) replacing the TRQ with a simple tariff; and (6) specifying the market access for Cuban sugar as part of an existing free-trade agreement (FTA) or a bilateral FTA with Cuba. If and when the United States does provide market access to Cuban sugar, it is unlikely that Cuban sugar production will ever achieve levels similar to those of the 1980s, which were predicated on Soviet demand. More likely is a scenario where Cuba exports some sugar to the United States, while focusing on the manufacture of sugarcane-based products such as rum, tafia, and perhaps even ethanol for both domestic and international markets.

A Complicated Relationship

The prospects for U.S.-Cuba agricultural trade depend on what policy measures the Cuban Government takes to foster further economic growth and development. A status quo scenario, in which the Government does little to modify its economic policies to complement the updated U.S. policy approach, is likely to result in some growth in U.S. agricultural exports to Cuba. U.S. exporters are uncertain about the extent to which the Cuban Government will decentralize the decisionmaking process for agricultural imports from the United States. Currently, all such imports must be routed through the government-operated Empresa Comercializadora de Alimentos (ALIMPORT—Food Trading Company), while agricultural imports from other supplying countries have other options (Gonzalez, 2013; Urban, 2015). However, the Cuban Government already has made some of its agricultural policies more market based, replacing large state farms with smaller cooperative production units, allowing the development of farmers' markets and at least one wholesale market for farmers, and securing foreign investment for the sugar sector (Messina, 2015; KurtzNicholl, 2011; Miroff, 2012; Frank, 2014).

A scenario featuring a broader opening of the Cuban economy to foreign trade and investment is likely to lead to more sustained growth of U.S.-Cuba agricultural trade, particularly if such an opening spurs income growth and the expansion of sectors that rely on imports, such as tourism, restaurants, food services, food manufacturing, and livestock production. The extent to which the Cuban Government maintains control over the economy will influence the pace of these changes. If the Government maintains a monopoly on official consumer and investment lending, for instance, the resulting allocation of financial capital may be inefficient and hamper economic growth. In this scenario, trade and investment still involve considerable startup costs, including time. Larger companies and investors are likely to have the resources necessary to navigate this process. Thus, the benefits of expanded trade and investment may accrue to larger firms with international experience and deeper pockets.

Still, the tourist economy and perhaps even the retirement economy are likely to expand in this scenario, as Cuba cultivates a reputation for being a safe place to visit and invest. Capital controls and the dual exchange rate would still limit the benefits that the average Cuban receives from trade and investment. In March 2014, the Cuban Government published the procedures that it will use to eliminate the dual exchange rate, but the precise date for implementing these plans has not yet been announced (Morris, 2015).

Alternatively, the Cuban Government could pursue more open trade and investment policies while favoring select groups currently or formerly associated with the Government. Tourism and imports would expand in this scenario, but exporters and investors would need to work through these select groups. Cuba's dual exchange rate would further allow these groups to capture many of the gains from trade. Large U.S firms with experience in similar economies are likely to find that they can trade and invest in Cuba in this scenario. The extent to which this new economic activity raises the incomes of Cuba's broader population would determine the impact of such growth on agricultural imports, particularly those of higher value.

The availability of credit will limit the pace at which the Cuban economy and Cuba's agricultural trade grow. In August 2014, Moody's lowered the credit rating for Cuba's sovereign debt from Caa1 to Caa2, due to concerns about the soundness of the Venezuelan economy—which supplies petroleum to Cuba under favorable terms of financing—and concerns about succession planning for Cuba's leadership (Tamayo, 2014). All three of the "Caa" categories (Caa1, Caa2, and Caa3) are used to indicate sovereign debt that is of low quality and high credit risk. Given this perception of low creditworthiness, a boom-and-bust cycle—in which generous amounts of lending foster rapid growth in agricultural and nonagricultural imports, followed by difficulties in repaying these loans—seems unlikely.

Absent the election and inauguration of a democratically elected government in Cuba, which would trigger the Helms-Burton Act's procedures for suspending and then ending the U.S. economic embargo on Cuba, further congressional action is needed to define the policy framework for establishing a more normal economic relationship with Cuba. Actions that might stimulate U.S. agricultural exports to Cuba include a loosening of restrictions on private-sector credit for Cuban purchases of U.S. agricultural products and allowing Cuba to export products (agricultural and nonagricultural) to the United States, which would enable Cuba to accumulate the foreign exchange needed to import more.

Over the long term, fostering growth in U.S.-Cuba agricultural trade hinges on building a foundation for a two-way relationship in trade and investment and then creating the trust to sustain that relationship. For agricultural trade, that foundation does not yet exist as of now. While the United States over the past 15 years has quickly reestablished itself as one of Cuba's leading suppliers of agricultural imports, the updated U.S. policy approach to Cuba so far provides scant opportunities for Cuba to export agricultural products to the United States. Over the next 15 years, the challenge will be to provide more balanced opportunities for U.S.-Cuba agricultural trade and to continue to build U.S. and Cuban confidence in the emerging commercial relationship.

References

Website addresses current as of June 8, 2015, unless otherwise indicated.

Alvarez, José. 2013. "Transformations in Cuban Agriculture after 1959." University of Florida, Institute for Food and Agricultural Sciences (IFAS), Electronic Data Information Source (EDIS) Document FE481. June. http://edis.ifas.ufl.edu/pdffiles/FE/FE48100.pdf.

____. 2004. "Antecedents of the Cuban Agricultural Policies of the 1990s." University of Florida, Institute for Food and Agricultural Sciences (IFAS),

Electronic Data Information Source (EDIS) Document FE485. July. http://edis.ifas.ufl.edu/pdffiles/FE/FE48500.pdf.

Bethel, Leslie (ed.). 1993. Cuba: A Short History. Cambridge, England, and New York: Cambridge University Press.

Birch, Georgia. 2015. "Is Cuba ready for the business boom?" The Telegraph (London). April 5. http://www.telegraph.co.uk/news/worldnews/central americaandthecaribbean/cuba/11514267/Is-Cuba-ready-for-the-business-boom.html.

Boughner, Devry, and Jonathan Coleman. 2002. "Normalizing Trade Relations with Cuba: GATT-compliant Options for the Allocation of the U.S. Sugar Tariff-rate Quota," Estey Centre Journal of International Law and Trade Policy 3(1):46-61. http://ageconsearch.umn.edu/bitstream/23911/1/03010046.pdf.

Central Intelligence Agency. 2015. The World Factbook. April 21. https://www.cia.gov/library/ publications/resources/the-world-factbook/.

Clinton, William J. 1996. "Statement on Signing the Cuban Liberty and Democratic Solidarity (LIBERTAD) Act of 1996." March 12. Online by Gerhard Peters and John T. Woolley, The American Presidency Project. http://www.presidency.ucsb.edu/ws/?pid=52532.

Coleman, Jonathan. 2009. U.S. Agricultural Sales to Cuba: Certain Economic Effects of U.S. Restrictions. An Update. U.S. International Trade Commission, Office of Industries Working Paper No. ID-22, June. http://www.usitc.gov/publications/332/ID-22.pdf.

Davis, Christopher G., David Harvey, Steven Zahniser, Fred Gale, and William Liefert. 2013. Assessing the Growth of U.S. Broiler and Poultry Meat Exports. U.S. Department of Agriculture, Economic Research Service, Outlook Report No. LPDM-231-01. Nov. http://www.ers.usda.gov/media/1217411/ldpm-231-01-with-keywords. pdf.

Dye, Alan, and Richard Sicotte. 2004. "The U.S. Sugar Program and the Cuban Revolution." The Journal of Economic History 64(3, Sept.): 673-704.
http://www.jstor.org/stable/3874816?seq=1#page_scan_tab_ contents.

Efferson, Norman J. 1952. The Production and Marketing of Rice, Simmons Press, New Orleans, Louisiana.

European Union Delegation to Cuba. 2015. Cuba and the EU: Political and Economic Relations. Webpage. http://eeas.europa.eu/delegations/cuba/eu_cuba/political_relations/index_en.htm.

Food and Agricultural Organization of the United Nations, Statistics Division. 2015. FAOSTAT. May. http://faostat3.fao.org/home/E.

Fletcher, Pascal. 1993. "Cuba Says U.S. Sanctions Will Hurt Trade," Reuters.

Frank, Marc. 2014. "Cuba experiments with wholesale market for farmers," Reuters. June 1. http://www.reuters.com/article/2014/06/01/us-cuba-reform-agriculture-idUSKBN0EC1NW20140601.

_____. 2013. "Cuba reports sugar production rose 8 percent, lower than expected." Reuters. June 17. http://www.reuters.com/article/2013/06/17/food-cuba-sugar-idUSL2N0ET0FV20130617.

Franklin, Jane. 1997. Cuba and the United States—A Chronological History. Melbourne: Ocean Press.

Global Trade Information Services. 2015. Global Trade Atlas. Columbia, South Carolina.

Gonzalez, Omar. 2013. Cuba: Food and Agricultural Import Regulations and Standards – Narrative: FAIRS Country Report. U.S. Department of Agriculture, Foreign Agricultural Service, Global Agricultural Information Network Report No. CB1315. December 3. http://gain.fas.usda.gov/Recent%20GAIN%20Publications/Food%20and%20Agricultural%20Import%20Regulations%20and%20Standards%20-%20Narrative_Miami%20ATO_Cuba_12-5-2013.pdf.

Grogg, Patricia. 2013. "Cuban Sugar Sector Aims for Recovery in 2013." Inter Press Service News Agency. Jan. 9. http://www.ipsnews.net/2013/01/cuban-sugar-sector-aims-for-recovery-in-2013/.

The Guardian. 1961. "US Breaks with Cuba: Embassy Official Arrested." Jan. 3. http://www.theguardian.com/world/from-the-archive-blog/2014/dec/17/how-us-cuba-relations-broke-down-guardian-archive.

_____. 1960. "U.S. Bans Exports to Cuba." October 20. http://www.theguardian.com/world/from-the-archive-blog/2014/dec/17/how-us-cuba-relations-broke-down-guardian-archive.

Guida, Victoria. 2015. "For Businesses, Road to Cuba Fraught with Uncertainties," Politico. March 10.

Haney, Patrick Jude, and Walt Vanderbush. 2005. The Cuban Embargo: The Domestic Politics of an American Foreign Policy. Pittsburgh: University of Pittsburgh Press. http://digital.library.pitt. edu/cgi-bin/t/text/text-idx?c=pittpress;cc=pittpress;view=toc;idno=31735062136647.

Harris, Terry L. 2015. "Statement of Terry L. Harris, Senior Vice President, Marketing & Rick Management, Riceland Foods, Inc., to the U.S. International Trade Commission." June 2.

Holder, Shelby H., and Warren R. Grant. 1979. U.S. Rice Industry. U.S. Department of Agriculture, Economic Statistics and Cooperative Service, Agricultural Economic Report No. 433. Aug.

Hufbauer, Gary Clyde, Jeffrey J. Schott, Kimberly Ann Elliott, and Milica Cosic. 2011. Case Studies in Economic Sanctions and Terrorism: Case 60-3: US v. Cuba (1960–: Castro). October. http://www.iie.com/publications/papers/sanctions-cuba-60-3.pdf.

Kandell, Jonathan. 2015. "As Cuba-U.S. Relations Thaw, Remittances Stoke New Tensions," Institutional Investor. April 2. http://www.institutionalinvestor.com/article/3442249/asset-management-macro/as-cuba-us-relations-thaw-remittances-stoke-new-tensions.html#. VWzL7mwpC70.

Kost, William E. 2004a. "Cuban Agriculture: To Be or Not to Be Organic?" Cuba in Transition: Volume 14. Papers and Proceedings of the Fourteenth Annual Meeting of the Association for the Study of the Cuban Economy: 274-281. http://www.ascecuba.org/c/wp-content/uploads/2014/09/v14-kost.pdf.

_____. 2004b. Cuba's Citrus Industry: Growth and Change. U.S. Department of Agriculture, Economic Research Service, Outlook Report No. FTS-309-01. April. http://webarchives.cdlib. org/sw1vh5dg3r/http://ers.usda.gov/publications/fts/APR04/fts30901/fts30901.pdf.

_____. 2004c. Cuba's Tropical Fruit Industry. U.S. Department of Agriculture, Economic Research Service, Outlook Report No. FTS-309-02. April. http://www.ers.usda.gov/media/1719988/fts30902.pdf.

Krinsky, Michael, and David Golove. 1993. United States Economic Measures Against Cuba: Proceedings in the United Nations and International Law Issues. Northampton, MA: Aletheia Press.

Kurtz-Nicholl, Jesse. 2011. "Cuban Pesos: A Farmer's Market Experience." Webpage, Center for a Livable Future. Jan. 21. http://www.livablefutureblog.com/2011/01/cuban-pesos-a-famer%E2%80%99s-market-experience.

Mears, Leon G. 1962. Agriculture and Food Situation in Cuba. U.S. Department of Agriculture, Economic Research Service. May. https://archive.org/details/agriculturefoods28mear.

Menéndez, Fernando. 2015. "The 'New Normal' in Cuba, U.S. and China Relations," China-U.S. Focus. Jan. 21. http://www.chinausfocus.com/foreign-policy/the-new-normal-in-cuba-u-s-and-china-relations/.

Messina, William A. 2015. "The Cuban Factor." Webinar. Feb. 4. http://www.piecenter.com/2015/01/28/hot-topic-webinar-the-cuban-factor-agricultural-trade-with-cuba/.

Miroff, Nick. 2012. "In Farmers Market, A Free Market Rises In Cuba." National Public Radio. Dec. 7. http://www.npr.org/blogs/thesalt/2012/12/07/166676952/in-farmers-market-a-free-market-rises-in-cuba.

Morris, Emily. 2015. "How Will U.S.-Cuban Normalization Affect Economic Policy in Cuba?" Paper prepared for forum entitled "Scholarly Implications of Normalization: Scholarly Perspectives on U.S.-Cuban Relations," organized by the Center for Latin American and Latino Studies, American University, and the Social Science Research Council. April. http://www. american.edu/clals/upload/2015-AU-SSRC-Morris-How-will-US-Cuban-normalization-affecteconomic-policy-in-Cuba-FINAL.pdf.

National Milk Producers Federation and U.S. Dairy Export Council. 2010. Dairy Groups Support the Cuba Travel Restriction Reform and Export Enhancement Act. News release, February 24. http://www.nmpf.org/ print/435.

_____. 2009. U.S. Dairy Industry Groups Urge Passage of Cuba Trade Bills. News release, May 21. http://www.cuba-l.com/us-dairy-industry-groups-urge-passage-of-cuba-trade-bills/.

Oxford University Press. 2015. Oxford Dictionaries. Webpages. http://www. oxforddictionaries. com/us/definition/american_english/rum and http://www.oxforddictionaries.com/us/definition/american_english/ tafia.

Parlapiano, Alicia. 2014. "How America's Relationship with Cuba Will Change," New York Times, Dec, 17. http://www.nytimes.com/ interactive/2014/12/17/world/americas/cuba-sanctions.html.

República de Cuba, Oficina Nacional de Estadísticas, Dirección de Agropecuario. 2010. Siembra y Superficie Existente Sembrada de Arroz: Año 2009. Febrero. http://www.one.cu/publicaciones/05agropecuario/ arroz/PubElectArrozDic2009.pdf.

Rey Mellén, Patricia. 2014. "China And Cuba: Skip the Ideology, Let's Talk About Money," International Business Times. April 24. http://www.ibtimes.com/china-cuba-skip-ideology-lets-talk-about-money-1575560.

Romanò, Sara, and Dayma Echevarría León. 2015. "La Inserción en el Cuentapropismo en Cuba: El Papel de los Contactos Personales y de la Afiliación al Partido Comunista." Paper prepared for delivery at the 2015 Congress of the Latin American Studies Association, San Juan, Puerto Rico, May 27-30.

Ross, James E. 2004. "Cuba: U.S. Agribusiness Export Prospects Under Three Scenarios," Cuba in Transition: Volume 14. Papers and Proceedings of the Fourteenth Annual Meeting of the Association for the Study of the Cuban Economy: 369-380. http://www.ascecuba.org/c/wp-content/uploads/2014/ 09/v14-ross.pdf.

Rosson, Parr, Flynn Adcock, Eric Manthei. 2010. Estimated Economic Impacts of the Travel Restriction Reform and Export Enhancement Act of 2010. Texas A&M University, Center for North American Studies (CNAS) Report No. 2010-01. March. http://cnas.tamu.edu/Publications/4645%20Tourism/Estimated%20Impacts%20of%20HR%204645%20B.pdf.

Solomon, Daniel P. 2011. Breaking Up with Cuba: The Dissolution of Friendly Relations Between Washington and Havana, 1956-1961. Jefferson, North Carolina, and London: McFarland & Company, Inc.

Sullivan, Mark P. 2014. Cuba: U.S. Restrictions on Travel and Remittances. Congressional Research Report No. RL31139. August 19. http://fas.org/sgp/crs/row/RL31139.pdf.

Tamayo, Juan O. 2014a. "Russia-Cuba love affair on again." Miami Herald. July 19. http://www. miamiherald.com/news/nation-world/world/americas/article1976207.html.

_____. 2014b. "Moody cuts Cuba's credit rating." Miami Herald. April 28. http://www.miamiherald.com/news/nation-world/world/americas/article1963556.html (accessed March 17, 2015).

United Nations, Department of Economic and Social Affairs, Statistics Division. 2015. UN Comtrade: International Trade Database. http://comtrade.un.org/data/.

United Nations Environment Programme. 2015. "Green Environment Success Stories: Organic Agriculture in Cuba." Webpage. http://www.unep.org/greeneconomy/SuccessStories/OrganicAgricultureinCuba/tabid/29890/Default.aspx.

U.S. Dairy Export Council. 2015. Backgrounder: Trade with Cuba. http://usdec.files.cms-plus.com/PDFs/TradePolicy/Trade_With_Cuba.pdf.

U.S. Department of Agriculture, Agriculture Marketing Service (USDA/AMS). 1956. The Rice Situation: 1957 Outlook Issue, RS-1. Nov. 29.

U.S. Department of Agriculture, Foreign Agricultural Service (USDA/FAS). 2015a. Global Agricultural Trade System (GATS). Interactive database. http://apps.fas.usda.gov/gats/

_____. 2015b. "Product Groups: FATUS." Webpage. http://apps.fas.usda.gov/gats/ProductGroup. aspx?GROUP=FATUS.

_____. 2015c. Production, Supply and Distribution Online. Interactive database. http://apps.fas. usda.gov/psdonline.

_____. 1959. Foreign Agricultural Trade of the United Stat.es: Trade by Countries for Fiscal Year 1957-58. March.

_____. 1958. Foreign Agricultural Trade of the United States: Trade by Countries for Fiscal Year 1956-57. Jan.

_____. 1957. Foreign Agricultural Trade of the United States: Trade by Countries for Fiscal Year 1955-56. Jan.

U.S. Department of Agriculture, Foreign Agricultural Service, Office of Global Analysis. 2008. Cuba's Food & Agriculture Situation Report. March. http://www.ilfb.org/media/546435/fas_ report_on_cuba.pdf.

U.S. Department of Commerce, Bureau of the Census. 2013. International Data Base. Dec. 19. http://www.census.gov/population/international/data/idb/informationGateway.php.

U.S. Department of Commerce, International Trade Administration. 2012. Trade Finance Guide: A Quick Reference for U.S. Exporters. Nov. http://export.gov/TradeFinanceGuide/

U.S. Department of State, Bureau of Public Affairs, Office of the Historian. 2015. "A Guide to the United States' History of Recognition, Diplomatic, and Consular Relations, by Country, since 1776: Cuba." Webpage. http://history.state.gov/countries/cuba.

_____. 2013a. "Milestones: 1961-1968: The Bay of Pigs Invasion and its Aftermath, April 1961- October 1962." Webpage. https://history.state.gov/milestones/1961-1968/bay-of-pigs.

_____. 2013b. "Milestones: 1961-1968: The Cuban Missile Crisis, October 1962." Webpage. https://history.state.gov/milestones/1961-1968/cuban-missile-crisis.

U.S. Department of State, Bureau of Western Hemisphere Affairs. 2013. "U.S. Relations with Cuba: Fact Sheet." Webpage. Aug. 30. http://www.state.gov/r/pa/ei/bgn/2886.htm.

U.S. International Trade Commission (USITC). 2007. U.S. Agricultural Sales to Cuba: Certain Economic Effects of U.S. Restrictions. U.S. International Trade Commission Publication No. 3932. July. http://www.usitc.gov/publications/332/pub3932.pdf.

_____. 2001. The Economic Impact of U.S. Sanctions with Respect to Cuba. U.S. International Trade Commission Publication No. 3398. Feb. http://www.usitc.gov/publications/industry_econ_ analysis_332/2001/economic_impact_us_sanctions_respect_cuba.htm.

U.S. Statutes at Large. 2000. Trade Sanctions Reform and Export Enhancement Act of 2000. Title IX of Public Law 106-387. http://www.gpo.gov/fdsys/pkg/STATUTE-114/pdf/STATUTE114-Pg1549.pdf.

_____. 1996. Cuban Liberty and Democratic Solidarity (LIBERTAD) Act of 1996. Public Law 104-114. http://www.gpo.gov/fdsys/pkg/STATUTE-110/pdf/STATUTE-110-Pg785.pdf.

Urban, Peter. 2015. "Riceland Foods Seeks Trade with Cuba," Arkansas News. April 21. http://arkansasnews.com/news/arkansas/riceland-foods-seeks-trade-cuba.

Whitefield, Mimi. 2015. "U.S. and Cuban diplomats meet in Havana for third round of talks," Miami Herald. March 16. http://www.miamiherald.com/news/nation-world/world/americas/cuba/article14570231.html.

White House, Office of the Press Secretary. 2014. Fact Sheet: Charting a New Course on Cuba. Press release, Dec. 17. https://www.whitehouse.gov/the-press-office/2014/12/17/fact-sheet-charting-new-course-cuba.

Wilkinson, Tracy, and Vincent Bevins. 2015. "In funding Cuba port project, Brazil set to gain key foothold," Los Angeles Times. Feb. 17. http://www.latimes.com/world/brazil/la-fg-ff-cubamariel-20150217-story.html#page=1.

Wong, Kam S. 1994. "The Cuban Democracy Act of 1992: The Extraterritorial Scope of Section 1706(a)," University of Pennsylvania Journal of International Business Law 14(4):651-82. https://www.law.upenn.edu/journals/jil/articles/volume14/issue4/Wong14U.Pa.J.Int'lBus.L.651(1993).pdf.

World Bank. 2015a. "Data: Indicators: GDP per capita (current US$)." World Bank Open Data. Website: http://data.worldbank.org/indicator/NY.GDP.PCAP.CD.

_____. 2015b. "How do you define remittances?" Webpage. https://datahelpdesk.worldbank.org/knowledgebase/articles/114950-how-do-you-define-remittances.

Yonhap News Agency. 2015. "S. Korean trade insurer establishes credit line with Cuba." Feb. 10. http://english.yonhapnews.co.kr/business/2015/02/09/8/0502000000AEN20150209011600320F. html.

Zepeda, Lydia. 2003. "Cuban Agriculture: A Green & Red Revolution." Choices Magazine. 4th Quarter. http://www.choicesmagazine.org/2003-4/2003-4-01.htm.

End Notes

[1] In this report, we define agricultural trade as encompassing those commodities and products within the Foreign Agricultural Trade of the United States (FATUS) classification scheme, as specified by USDA/FAS (2015b).

[2] The fiscal year of the U.S. Federal Government runs from October 1 to September 30. Thus, FY 2015 began on October 1, 2014, and will end on September 30, 2015. FY 1956-58 were the last 3 FYs prior to the collapse of the prerevolutionary government in January 1959 and correspond to the period when the revolutionaries pressed their attack.

[3] Cuba averaged 56 kilograms per capita in 1957, obtained by dividing the sum of Cuba's domestic production and imports of rice for 1957, as reported by Mears (1962), by Cuba's population in 1957, as estimated by U.S. Department of Commerce, Bureau of the Census (2013). Cuba's pre-revolutionary rice production peaked in 1957, as the harvest of the subsequent year's main crop was interrupted by the armed conflict.

[4] U.S. rice exports to Cuba picked up sharply during World War II, when shipments from Cuba's previous top suppliers—Burma and Thailand—were suspended due to the war. Prior to the late 1930s, the United States had been only a minor supplier of rice to Cuba. From the mid-1940s up until the embargo, the United States supplied the bulk of Cuba's rice imports (Efferson, 1952: 518-521).

[5] The imported molasses was used primarily to produce industrial alcohol, according to a statement in 1960 by a USDA spokesperson (*The Guardian*, 1960).

[6] For summaries of the political and military confrontations between the United States and Cuba during the late 1950s and early 1960s, see U.S. Department of State, Bureau of Public Affairs, Office of the Historian (2013a, 2013b, 2015).

[7] Haney and Vanderbush (2005) discuss the policy context that led to the passage of the Helms-Burton Act.

[8] Each of these six commodities accounted for at least $10 million in exports to Cuba during at least 1 year during 2000-11.

[9] The USITC (2007: 3-8 to 3-12) illustrates the difference between these two techniques using U.S. agricultural exports to Cuba and to the Dominican Republic as contrasting examples.

[10] See, for instance, Harris (2015) and National Milk Producers Federation (2009).

[11] Rum is "an alcoholic liquor distilled from sugar-cane residues or molasses," while tafia is a "drink similar to rum, distilled from molasses or waste from the production of brown sugar" (Oxford University Press, 2015). USDA's definition of agricultural trade considers beer, wine, and unmanufactured tobacco to be agricultural products, but not rum, other distilled spirits, and tobacco products such as cigars and cigarettes.

[12] In this section, we use a summary by Parlapiano (2014) to identify those elements within the updated U.S. approach, as described by the White House (2014), that are new and not implemented previously.

[13] Already on the list of classifications requiring only a general license in order to travel to Cuba are: family visits; official business of the U.S. Government, foreign governments, and certain intergovernmental organizations; journalistic activity; professional research and professional meetings; educational activities; and religious activities.

[14] The World Bank (2015b) provides a more thorough definition: "Personal remittances are the sum of personal transfers and compensation of employees.... Personal transfers include all current transfers in cash or in kind between resident and nonresident individuals, independent of the source of income of the sender (and regardless of whether the sender receives income from labor, entrepreneurial or property income, social benefits, and any

other types of transfers; or disposes assets) and the relationship between the households (regardless of whether they are related or unrelated individuals). Compensation of employees refers to the income of border, seasonal, and other short-term workers who are employed in an economy where they are not resident and of residents employed by nonresident entities."

[15] The U.S. Department of Commerce's International Trade Administration (2012:4) defines the cash-in-advance payment method as when "payment is received before the ownership of the goods is transferred."

[16] Cuba's gross domestic product (GDP) is challenging to estimate due to the presence of market and nonmarket elements in the Cuban economy. According to the World Bank (2015a), Cuba's GDP per capita was about $6,100 in 2013, and the Dominican Republic's was about $5,700, without accounting for cross-country differences in purchasing power.

[17] The deepwater Port of Mariel is being renovated amid the construction of an adjacent industrial zone. This project will cost about $1 billion and is being funded primarily by the Brazilian Development Bank (BNDES), which is providing about $700 million of the financing (Wilkinson and Bevins, 2015).

[18] Although Mexican sugar exports to the United States are free from tariff and quota restrictions under NAFTA, they face separate quantity and price limits as part of a December 2014 agreement between the U.S. and Mexican Governments that suspended U.S. antidumping and countervailing duty investigations concerning sugar imports from Mexico. In April 2015, however, the U.S. Department of Commerce announced that it would resume these investigations in response to appeals filed by two sugarcane refining companies.

In: Agricultural Trade Between the U.S. and Cuba ISBN: 978-1-63484-430-7
Editor: Lana Valdez

Chapter 3

WHERE TO NEXT FOR CUBAN FOOD AND AGRICULTURE*

Samuel D. Wilton

REPORT HIGHLIGHTS

In December 2014 the United States embarked on a new diplomatic journey with Cuba, in the process rejuvenating U.S. agriculture's interest in our southern neighbor. U.S. agriculture has high expectations because of Cuba's proximity to the United States. Despite the recent changes, Cuba's economic environment presents many challenges. This report summarizes the U.S. – Cuba agricultural trade relationship and Cuba's current describes Cuba's market potential for U.S. agriculture.

I. INTRODUCTION

On July 20, 2015, after more than fifty years without formal diplomatic relations, Cuba and the United States re-opened their embassies. This was one of many steps the United States and Cuba must take to restore normal relations. Additional support from the U.S. Congress is needed in order to

* This is an edited, reformatted and augmented version of Global Agricultural Information Network Report Number CB1515, issued by the USDA Foreign Agricultural Service, October 23, 2015.

fully restore relations. The gradual thaw of relations between the United States and Cuba opens many opportunities for U.S. agriculture. This report will outline how U.S. suppliers can legally position themselves in the Cuban market while reducing financial risks.

This report will first recap U.S.-Cuban relations since the second half of the 20th century. Next it will describe the Cuban market, and Cuban consumption habits goods. It will then talk about steps the American government is considering taking, including bills different members of Congress have proposed, and what the removal of sanctions might mean for US-Cuba trade. Lastly, it will make the point that even as political relations thaw, tension between the two countries still exists. Trade can and does exist between countries on less than friendly political terms, but it does somewhat impede trade. This will likely be the case for the United States and Cuba's trading relationship.

II. American-Cuban Relations 1959-2015

The state of the Cuban agricultural sector has closely tracked Cuba's political fortunes abroad. The sector's productivity plummeted after the Cuban Revolution and the subsequent U.S. economic sanctions. Cuban agriculture received a boost when the Soviet Union bought Cuban sugar at three times the world price in exchange for desperately-needed oil and machinery. When the Soviet Union collapsed, Cuban exports declined nearly 80 percent overnight.

The impact on Cuban agriculture was dramatic. Without sufficient inputs, large farming operations ground to a halt. The impact on food consumption paralleled production with the average caloric intake estimated to have fallen from approximately 3,000 calories a day to somewhere between 1,400 and 2,400, which included a 40 percent drop in the amount of protein consumed. After an initial period of intense hardship, the Cuban economy slowly began to recover. A new State sponsor arrived in the form of President Hugo Chavez' Socialist Bolivarian Republic which heralded the resumption of subsidized oil under the PetroCaribe program, which continues today. In more recent times, the Venezuelan government has supplied the Cuban government with petroleum in exchange for service of Cuban medical providers. In 2000, U.S. President Bill Clinton signed into law the Trade Sanctions Reform and Export Enhancement Act that tightened overall sanction terms and conditions but exempted U.S. agricultural and medical products. Following Hurricane

Michelle in 2001, U.S. agricultural exports began flowing into Cuba, recording a 42 percent market share by 2009 before dropping to just 16 percent in 2014.

III. The Cuban Market

Cuba is a tale of two markets, pre- and post-Castro. Before the Communist revolution, Cuba supplied the United States with many agricultural products, most prominent of which was sugar. Tobacco and citrus crops also played a role. During the 1930s, the United States generated 75 percent of Cuba's export revenue, which all ground to a halt with implementation of the U.S. embargo in 1959. Cuba depended upon agricultural exports to the United States to generate much-needed foreign cash reserves. Cuba also depended on U.S. agricultural imports to feed its population. For example, pre-embargo Cuba represented the number one market for U.S. rice. After the Revolution, the state played a dominant role in the agricultural industry by nationalizing holdings of all large farmers, and centralizing production planning. Cuban farmers were required to contribute a certain percentage of their harvest to the state, and had no input on valuation of their commodities. These changes left Cuban agriculture production in a precarious state as it dampened producer incentives.

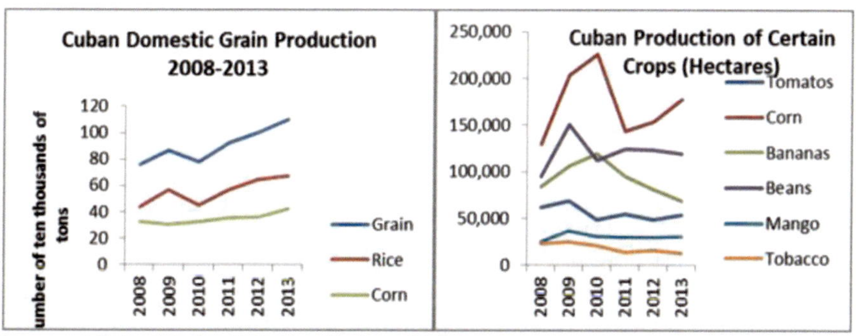

Source: Oficina Nacional de Estadísticas (Cuba).

According to the CIA World Fact book, the Cuban infrastructure to support the country's commerce consists of: 60,858 km of roadway (of which 29,820 km are paved), 8,203 km of railway (of which 8,134 km are standard gauge), 133 airports (2013) (of which 64 have paved runways), and eight major seaports, Aside from the Ports of Havana and Mariel, the latter which will be able to welcome post Panamax ships in 2016, Cuban ports lack dry and cold storage capacity, port depth, and efficient offloading capabilities.

Cuban land is also in poor condition. Cuban agronomist María Cruz wrote in a 2007 article that 75 percent of Cuba's farmland was degraded to some degree; 3 million hectares (45 percent) were low in fertility, 4.6 million hectares (69 percent) were low in organic matter, and 2.5 million hectares and 1 million hectares (15 percent), exhibited medium to severe erosion respectively.

Roughly 60 percent of all Cuban land is arable. Sugar cane represented a little under a third of Cuba's agricultural production, down from nearly two thirds in 1990. Cuba's biggest production crops are, ranked in descending importance, sugar cane, vegetables and melons, cereals, and tropical fruit.

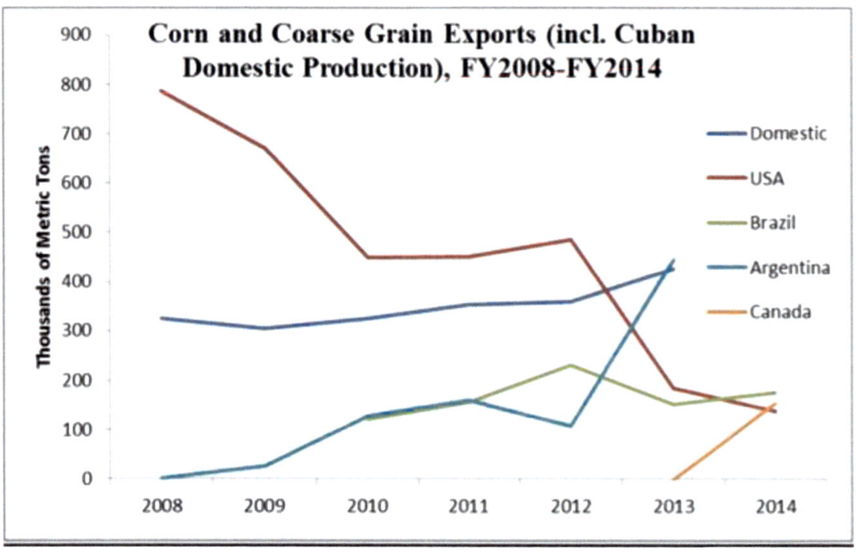

Source: USDA/FAS Global Agricultural Trade System, Global Trade Atlas, Oficina Nacional de Estadísticas (Cuba).

Inclement weather, in particular hurricanes intermixed with periodic droughts, frequently limits Cuba's agricultural production. Since 2001, 16 tropical storms or hurricanes have directly landed on Cuba. In 2001 Hurricane Dennis, a Category 4 Storm devastated Cuban agriculture production to the point that the country had to import over $4 million worth of food and agricultural products in the last six weeks of that year (Reference Messina). The storm deprived over 20 percent of the Cuban population of running water for several months. In 2012 Hurricane Sandy left a similar path of destruction across the island.

The droughts that have occurred appear when El Nino warms the Pacific waters that affect wind patterns across the region. In 2004 the worst drought then recorded in history reduced the country's water supplies leading to over one million people dependent solely on government water deliveries for many months. "The period from January (2015) up to the present (through August) has been the driest in terms of precipitation since 1901," per Cuba's state-run waterworks department. At the end of September 2015 Cuba's reservoirs were reported at about 35 percent of capacity, and in some provinces, they have run well below 20 percent. Of the country's 242 reservoirs, 25 were completely dry, and with just two months left for the rainy season, Cuban authorities had taken the drastic steps to seed clouds. Under such unpredictable weather patterns, focus on crop production has given way to basic survival in recent years.

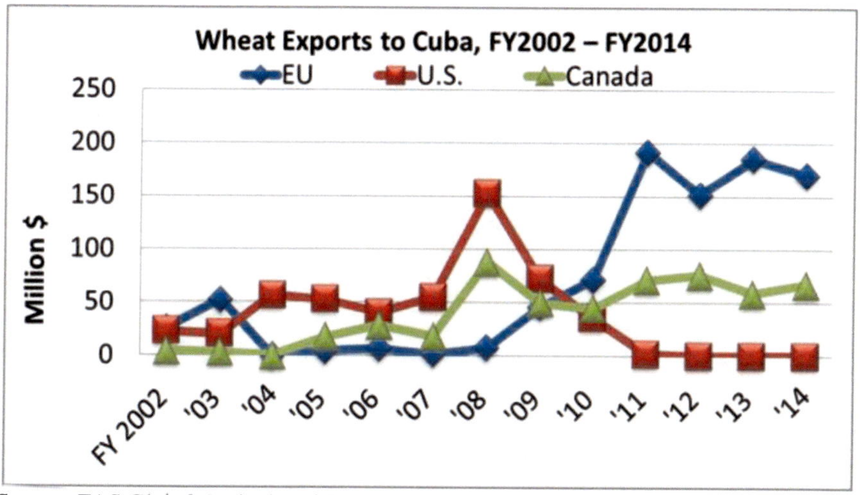

Source: FAS Global Agricultural Trade System, Global Trade Atlas.

The Cuban food market is heavily dependent on imports, creating an attractive environment for U.S. exporters. In 2014, for example, Cuba imported over $200 million of wheat. As background, between 2004 and 2009, the United States was Cuba's largest supplier of wheat, supplying on average, and $260 million per year. Likewise, the United States was Cuba's principal supplier of corn until 2013, reaching a high of 810,000 Metric Tons (MT) valued at $180 million in 2008. Brazilian and Argentinian sources, combined with increased domestic production, have eroded U.S. market share. The United States export patterns of soybean and soybean meal to Cuba follow similar patterns. Between 2004 and 2009 the U.S. average annual exports of soybeans topped 127 MMT with a value of $43 million, while soybean meal equaled 136 MMT with a value of $39 million. In 2014, U.S. soybean exports totaled 57 MMT valued at $31 million, while soybean meal equaled 129 MMT valued at $67 million. Cuba, for its part, produces tropical fruit, seafood, tobacco, and sugar for export.

In the case of sugar, Cuba has a history of boom and bust in which preferential prices led to a massive buildup in production that inevitably crashed when support prices disappeared. At various times, the United States and the Soviet Union bought Cuban sugar at above-market rates. At present, Cuba has no such trade partner, thus production is correspondingly low at 1.6 Million Metric Tons (MMT) in 2013. In contrast from 1978 to 1991 annual production averaged over 7.2 MMT per year.

Other potential export crops for Cuba are dry beans and peas, lentils, and potatoes.

Euromonitor reports that Cuban food service consumption is on the increase. Between 2009 and 2014 Cubans consumed two million tons more food service items and purchased 36,000 tons more of foodservice packaged food.

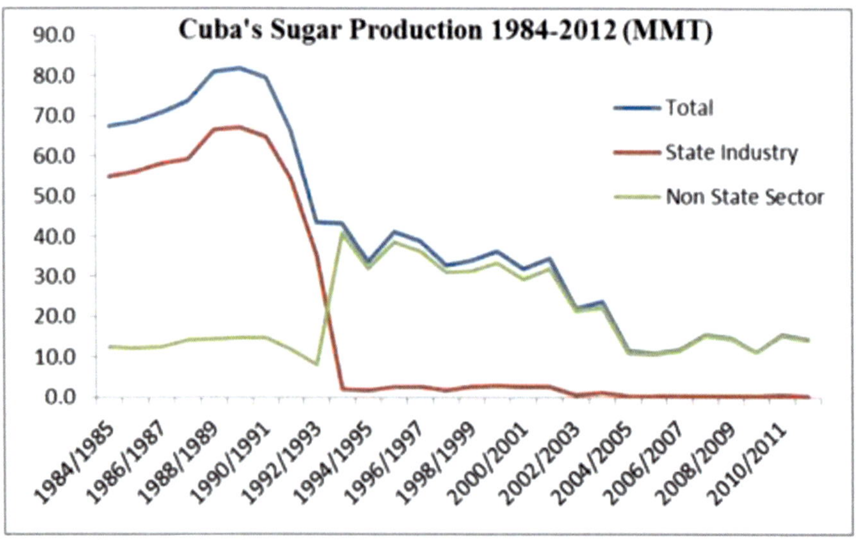

Source: Oficina Nacional de Estadísticas (Cuba).

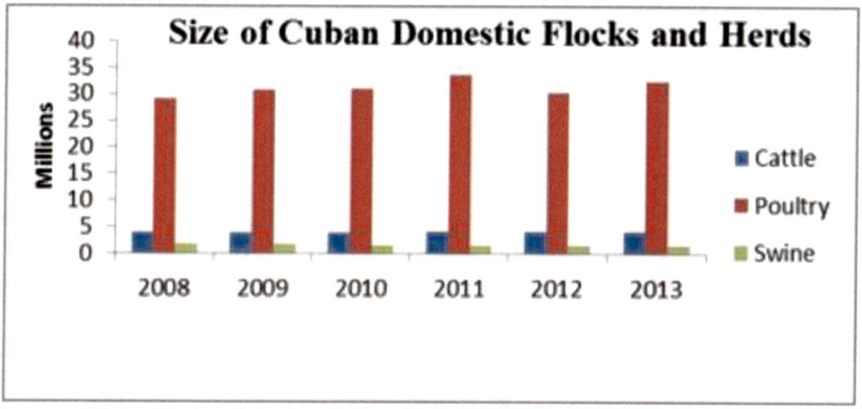

Source: Oficina Nacional de Estadísticas (Cuba).

The Cuban government has initiated "some" market reform. This involved distribution of the majority of public land to an assortment of small cooperatives, and the establishment of private agricultural markets for producers to sell surplus products after meeting their government set quota. President Raúl Castro's government strengthened the direction of these market-oriented reforms under a policy called *lineamientos* ("guidelines"). For many crops, production and yield have risen in tandem with producer's ability to market their surplus.

IV. Competitors

In July 2007, the U.S. International Trade Commission published a report titled "U.S. Agricultural Sales to Cuba: Certain Economic Effects of U.S. Restrictions." One section of the report looked at what might happen to U.S. agricultural exports, were sanctions to be lifted. Among other findings, it concluded that U.S. agricultural exports would increase for all major commodity groups except soybeans, and in particular with other food products, milk powder, processed foods, wheat, and other crops. The report runs through each sector, and how the removal of sanctions might change it. In 2007, when the report came out, the United States boasted a 33 percent market share of Cuban agricultural imports, more than double the European Union and Brazil's respective share of the market. In 2014 U.S. market share stood at 16 percent.

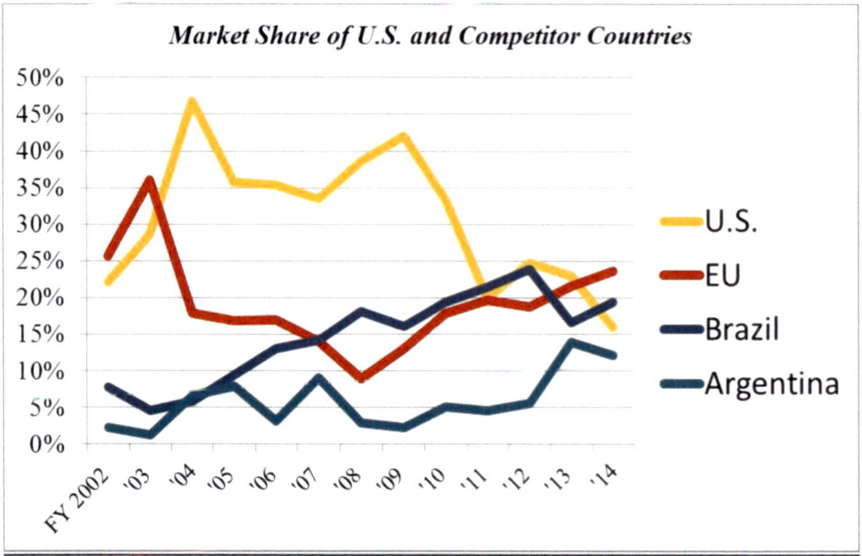

Source: FAS Global Agricultural Trade System, Global Trade Atlas.

While U.S. market share has been declining, competitor nations have increased their presence in Cuba. Brazil is financing $700 million of a nearly $1 billion Port of Mariel expansion project to better accommodate post Panamax ships, after completion of the Panama Canal expansion expected in the 2015-2016 period. In return for port financing provided by Brazil's development bank, it was agreed that at least $800 million would be spent on Brazilian goods and services.[1]

Since the early 1990s, the European Union (EU), as part of its outreach to Latin America and the Caribbean, has hosted rotating conferences. The latest such meeting took place in Brussels June 10-11, 2015. The CARIFORUM is the body that comprises Caribbean African, Caribbean and Pacific (ACP) states for the purpose of promoting and coordinating policy dialogue, cooperation and regional integration with the European Union. Cuba is one of 16 Participating State. In that regard, Cuba benefits directly from regional resources under Caribbean Regional Indicative Programs financed by the European Development Fund (EDF). The 11th European Development Fund (EDF) Caribbean Regional Indicative Program (CRIP) is valued at €346 million and provides for a significant allocation for Regional Economic Cooperation and Integration. The 11th EDF for the Caribbean region will run from 2014-2020 with a total funding of €1 billion.[2] The CARIFORUM group also belongs to the preferential trade arrangement with the European Union.

Cuba is also a member of the Bolivarian Alliance, an eleven member association, which started as an agreement between Cuba and Venezuela to exchange Venezuelan oil for Cuban medical assistance. In 2006, the last year for which Cuba has released total trade information; China was Cuba's largest trading partner. The 2013 incident wherein old Soviet weaponry was intercepted enroot to Pyongyang from Havana highlighted that some cooperation existed between North Korea and Cuba. In September 2015 the agriculture ministers of Argentina and Cuba signed a bilateral cooperation agreement for the next five years. The agreement focuses on food security, health and safety, and will involve joint ventures, technical cooperation and commercial contracts for livestock, animal products, arable and vegetable products, according to Argentina's agricultural ministry. For the livestock sector, added-value meats (poultry, pig and beef) will be covered, as well as nutrition and management of dairy cattle and milk technology.

V. The United States

The U.S. legislature remains undecided whether to remove or strengthen Cuban sanctions. In 2015, Congress has debated various bills circulating on the hill with the more notable ones identified here. On Feb 12, Senator Amy Klobuchar (D-MI) introduced the *Freedom to Export to Cuba Act*, which would lift the embargo. However, Representative Chris Smith (R-NJ), introduced HR 1782, the *Cuba Human Rights Act of 2015*, which would forbid the U.S. government from making any changes until the "government of Cuba cease violating the human rights of the people of Cuba." On June 11, Senators Jerry Moran (R-KS) and Angus King (I-ME) introduced the *Cuba Trade Act of 2015*, which would permit private businesses to export goods and services to Cuba but would maintain the restriction on use of federal funds to underwrite trade. On July 28, Representatives Tom Emmer (R-MN) and Kathy Castor (D-FL) introduced the *Cuba Trade Act of 2015* in the House of Representatives, which would grant U.S. businesses the freedom to trade with Cuba, while protecting taxpayers from any risk associated with such trade. Representative Mario Diaz-Balart (R-FL), had shepherded three appropriation bills through the House that contained a provision that would prohibit the State Department from using funds to create an embassy in Cuba, and undo some other changes President Obama's executive order on Cuba put into action. The current Republican Congressional leadership is opposed to liberalizing relations with Cuba, even though a number of Republicans have supported engagement.

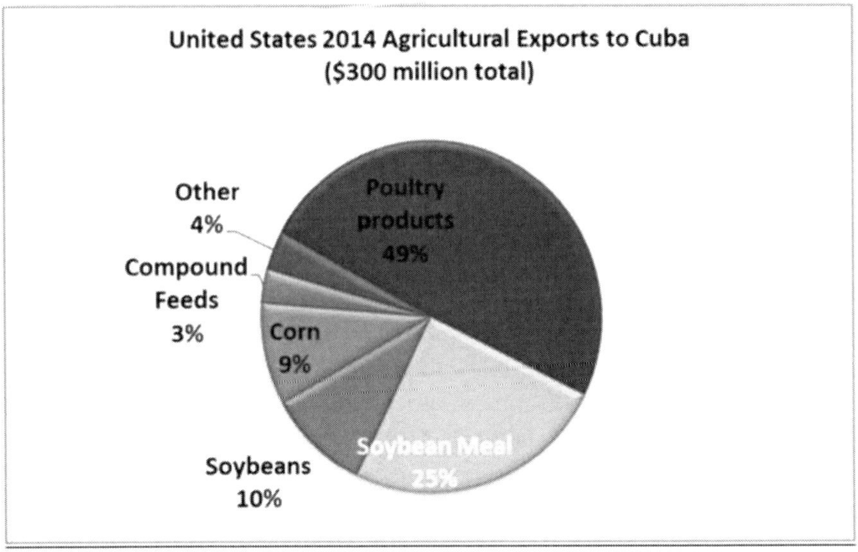

Source: USDA FAS Global Agricultural Trade System, Global Trade Atlas.

Several Senators—on the record—supporting rapprochement with Cuba, hail from states whose agricultural sector would benefit from normalization (two from Kansas, one each from Minnesota, Wyoming, Maine, and Arkansas). Other states with significant agricultural sectors that would benefit by normalization include: Louisiana (third biggest rice-producing state), Mississippi (fourth biggest rice-producing state), North Dakota (largest wheat-producing state), Montana (third largest wheat producing state), and Alabama (where the poultry industry represents 48 percent of agricultural exports).

The U.S. Agricultural Coalition for Cuba is a lobbying group dedicated to ending the U.S. trade embargo. The coalition is composed of various industry leaders—the National Barley Growers Association, the USA Rice Federation, the U.S. Meat Institute, and Cargill, among others. Cargill, which had $134.9 billion in revenue in 2014, is by far the largest of any company in these industries.

VI. Post Contact and Further Information

A. For more information on Cuba, please contact Post at:

Caribbean Basin Agricultural Trade Office Foreign Agricultural Service

United States Department of Agriculture
909 SE 1st Ave., Suite 720
Miami, FL 33131
Phone: (305) 536-5300
Fax: (305) 536-7577
E-mail: atocaribbeanbasin@fas.usda.gov

Staff:
Michael Henney, Director
Omar González, Agricultural Marketing Specialist Graciella Juelle, Agricultural Marketing Assistant

Please visit our website for more reports and information on the islands of the Caribbean Basin: http://www.cbato.fas.usda.gov

B. Select Cuban Government Agencies:

For a full explanation on Cuban import procedures and government contacts, please see: *Cuba's Food and Agricultural Import Regulations and Standards*

For general purchasing, documentation, and logistics issues related to the importation of bulk and intermediate U.S. agricultural products:

Empresa Cubana Importadora de Alimentos (Alimport)
Infanta #16, 3er Piso
Vedado, Plaza
La Habana, Cuba
Tel: [53] 836-9583 X135, X136, X137
E-mail: alimport@alimport.cu, aortiz@alimport.com.cu, secretarias@alimport.com.cu

For general purchasing, documentation, and logistics issues related to the importation of processed U.S. agricultural products:

Alimport MID
Calle 8 No. 508
E/5ta y 5ta B Playa
Tel: 011 (537) 204-1395/1274
Fax: 011 (537) 204-1395

For sanitary registration of food products and other food safety issues:
Instituto de Nutrición e Higiene de los Alimentos (Institute of Nutrition and Food Safety)
Ministerio de Salud Pública (Ministry of Public Health)
Infanta No. 1158 entre Llinás y Clavel
Centro Habana
Ciudad da la Habana, Cuba CP 10300
Tel: 011 (537) 878-1429, 878-1429, 878-5919, 870-5531 to 34

C. Select U.S. Government Agencies:

Office of Foreign Asset Control
United States Department of the Treasury
Treasury Annex
1500 Pennsylvania Ave., NW
Washington, DC 20220
Tel: [1] (800) 540-6322
Website: http://www.treasury.gov/about/organizational-structure/offices/Pages/Office-of-Foreign-Assets-Control.aspx
Office of Exporter Services Bureau of Industry and Security United States Department of Commerce Tel: (202) 482-4811
Website: https://www.bis.doc.gov/E-mail: ECDOEXS@bis.doc.gov

References

[1] CIA World Fact Book. Cuba. June 2015. https://www.cia.gov/library/publications/the-worldfactbook/geos/cu.html.

[2] Cloos, Kassondra. April 2013. The Pulitzer Center. Sustainable Farming in Cuba Ideal Cuba in an Isolated Country. http://www. huffingtonpost. com/2013/04/19/sustainable-farming-incuba n 3112088.html.

[3] Frank, Marc. March 2014. Reuters. Cuban sugar harvest falters; foreign investment sought. Reuters. http://www.reuters.com/article/2014/03/04/cuba-sugar-idUSL1N0M10TP20140304.

[4] Gonzalez, Omar. December 2014. "2014 Cuba Food and Agricultural Import Regulations and Standards – Narrative."

[5] Healy, Brian D., June 22, 2015 International Agricultural Trade Reports "U.S. Agricultural Exports to Cuba Have Substantial Room for Growth"

[6] Index Mundi. Sugar Monthly Price – US cents per Pound. http://www.indexmundi.com/commodities/?commodity=sugar&months=300.

[7] Karnowski, Steve. December 2014. Associated Press. US agriculture has big appetite for Cuba trade. http://www.denverpost.com/nationworld/ci 27168597/us-agriculture-has-big-appetite-cuba-trade.

[8] Kost, William. April 2004. Cuba's Citrus Industry: Growth and Change. United States Department of Agriculture. http://www.ers.usda.gov/media/1719994/fts30901.pdf.

[9] Leclair, Joshua. May 2015. Cuba's cooperative farms break new ground in production. Peoples World. http://peoplesworld.org/cuba-s-cooperative-farms-break-new-ground-in-production/.

[10] Lopez, Jessica. December 2013. Yale Global Health Review. Cuba: Agricultural Reform in the Special Period. http://yaleglobalhealth review.com/2013/12/01/evaluating-the-success-of-agriculturalreforms-on-health-during-the-special-period-in-cuba/.

[11] Messina, William. February 2015. Food and Resource Economics Department, University of Florida. The Cuban Factor: Agricultural Trade with Cuba. Powerpoint given to PIE Center webinar series.

[12] Office of Global Analysis, Foreign Agricultural Service, United States Department of Agriculture. March 2008. Cuba's Food & Agriculture Situation Report. http://www.ilfb.org/media/546435/fas report on cuba.pdf.

[13] Patel, Raj. April 2014. What Cuba Can Teach Us About Food and Climate Change? Slate Magazine. http://www.slate.com/articles/health and science/future tense/2012/04/agro ecology lessons from cuba on agriculture food and climate change.html.

[14] Peters, Philip. October 2012. Reforming Cuban Agriculture: Unfinished Business. Lexington Institute. http://www.american.edu/clals/upload/LexingtonCubanAgriculture-1.pdf.

[15] Quinn, Megan. February 2006. Resilience. The power of community: How Cuba survived peak oil. http://www.resilience.org/stories/2006-02-25/power-community-how-cuba-survived-peak-oil#.

[16] Schiffman, Richard. April 2013. How Cubans' Health Improved When Their Economy Collapsed. The Atlantic. http://www.theatlantic.com/health/archive/2013/04/how-cubans-health-improved-whentheir-economy-collapsed/275080/.

[17] Watson, Greg. April 2015. Boston Globe. Is Cuba the future of farming? https://www.bostonglobe.com/opinion/2015/04/15/cuba-future-farming/ESYROGF8WARyyRv3lmgNHO/story.html.

[18] Wexler, Alexandra. December 2014. U.S. Sugar Soars Above World Prices. Wall Street Journal. http://www.wsj.com/articles/u-s-sugar-soars-above-world-prices-1417999637.

[19] Wilkinson, Tracy and Bevins, Vincent. February 2015. In funding Cuba port project, Brazil set to gain key foothold. LA Times. http://www.latimes.com/world/brazil/la-fg-ff-cuba-mariel-20150217 - story.html.

[20] World Port Source. Port of Havana. http://www.worldport source.com/ports/commerce/CUB Port of Havana 1859.php.

[21] Zahniser, Steven and Cooke, Bryce et. al. June 2015. U.S.-Cuba Agricultural Trade: Past, Present, and Possible Future. Economic Research Service. United States Department of Agriculture. http://www.ers.usda.gov/publications/aes-outlook-for-us-agricultural-trade/aes-87.aspx.

End Notes

[1] "In funding Cuba port project, Brazil set to gain key foothold", LA Times 2/17/2015.

[2] July 15, 2015 Press release: Joint Communique – Third Meeting of the Joint CARIFORUM-EU Council.

In: Agricultural Trade Between the U.S. and Cuba ISBN: 978-1-63484-430-7
Editor: Lana Valdez

Chapter 4

STATEMENT OF MICHAEL SCUSE, UNDER SECRETARY, FARM AND FOREIGN AGRICULTURAL SERVICE, U.S. DEPARTMENT OF AGRICULTURE. HEARING ON "OPPORTUNITIES AND CHALLENGES FOR AGRICULTURE TRADE WITH CUBA"*

Chairman Roberts, Ranking Member Stabenow, and Members of the Committee, I am pleased to come before you today to discuss agricultural trade with Cuba. The Administration's new approach to Cuba is significant for U.S. agricultural producers, processors, and exporters. There are major opportunities for U.S. agriculture in Cuba, but significant challenges remain to doing business there.

CHARTING A NEW COURSE ON CUBA

As you know, on December 17, President Obama announced a set of policy and regulatory changes to chart a new course in U.S. relations with Cuba and to further engage and empower the Cuban people. As President

* This is an edited, reformatted and augmented version of a statement presented April 21, 2015 before the Senate Committee on Agriculture, Nutrition and Forestry.

Obama reiterated at the Summit of the Americas this month, the changes are aimed at giving Cuban citizens new opportunities to gain greater control over their own lives. The measures also seek to expand opportunities for America's farmers and ranchers to sell goods in Cuba.

Less than a month after the President's announcement, the Treasury Department's Office of Foreign Assets Control (OFAC) published amendments to the Cuban Assets Control Regulations (CACR) to implement the relevant policy changes. The regulatory changes removed certain technical barriers between the U.S. and Cuba and created a more efficient, less burdensome payment requirement and process for authorized sales of U.S. agricultural products to Cuba. These changes – which include a revised interpretation of the statutory term "cash-inadvance" as well as authorization for U.S. banks to establish correspondent accounts at Cuban banks – should improve the speed, efficiency, and oversight of authorized payments between the United States and Cuba. These changes had been sought by members of the U.S. agricultural community. Our belief is that, ultimately, they will help lead to expanded choices for Cuban consumers and an expanded customer base in Cuba for America's farmers and ranchers.

PERMITTED AGRICULTURAL SALES TO CUBA

Under the Trade Sanctions Reform and Export Enhancement Act of 2000 (TSRA), Congress lifted the ban on the export of agricultural products that had been restricted under Cuba sanctions for decades. Despite this opening, U.S. government agencies – including USDA – remain prohibited from providing government assistance, U.S. export assistance, and any U.S. credit or guarantees for exports to Cuba. As Secretary Vilsack has said, he can't use a single dollar of trade promotion funding for our trade with Cuba. These restrictions apply to FAS' successful cooperative market development programs like the Market Access Program and the Foreign Market Development Program.

The policy changes announced by the President are significant, but we still have legislative hurdles to cross. Legislation has been introduced to further open agricultural trade with Cuba, including legislation sponsored and cosponsored by members of this committee. USDA stands ready to provide technical assistance to you and other Members as Congress considers further openings with Cuba.

Cuba as a Potential Export Market

If the embargo is removed, we could be poised to become a major trading partner with Cuba. Cuba depends heavily on imports to feed its 11 million citizens and growing numbers of foreign visitors. According to the World Food Program, Cuba imports about 80 percent of its food, which means that the economic potential for our producers is significant. Unfortunately, the country is plagued with an outdated infrastructure, a depleted resource base, a lack of agricultural inputs, and has been subjected to devastating hurricanes. The United States has potentially huge structural advantages in exporting to Cuba. Chief among them is location. We are less than 100 miles away, meaning lower shipping costs and transit times, especially when compared to our current top competitors – Brazil and Europe. Plus, there's the fact that 11 million Cuban consumers desire food products that the United States can supply, and American agriculture wants to sell to Cuba.

Under TSRA, agricultural products are among a few types of goods that may be exported to Cuba under the longstanding U.S. embargo, and our producers have taken advantage of that opportunity. Before passage of TSRA, U.S. law prevented the sale of agricultural commodities to Cuba and agricultural sales were zero. By fiscal year 2008, U.S. agricultural exports to Cuba had reached a peak of $658 million. However, by the end of last fiscal year, they had fallen by more than half, to $300 million. Yet, at the same time, global agricultural exports to Cuba have doubled over the past decade to $1.7 billion.

Right now, the largest U.S. export to Cuba is poultry products, with exports valued at $148.1 million in FY 2014. This made Cuba the eighth-largest export market for U.S. poultry. Other top U.S. exports last fiscal year included soybean meal (valued at nearly $75 million), bulk soybeans (valued at more than $29 million), and bulk corn (valued at more than $28 million).

I am confident U.S. agricultural exporters can capture the market in Cuba, but I don't want to minimize the obstacles. In addition to those I've already talked about, here are a few more worth considering. Cuba is a country with limited foreign exchange. U.S. companies are also behind our foreign competitors in market development.

Another impediment to trade is Cuba's tightly controlled import policy requiring that all U.S. agricultural imports must be channeled through one state corporation, called Alimport. Many of our competitors have additional options of trading with other Cuban agencies, but Alimport is the exclusive agent for the Cuban government on buying decisions and negotiating purchases from U.S. firms. Alimport not only negotiates contracts for purchase with U.S. firms, but it arranges for payment, takes control of the imports at the Cuban port, and manages the distribution process within Cuba.

ENHANCING EXPORT OPPORTUNITIES AROUND THE GLOBE

The recent changes in U.S. policy toward Cuba are just one example of opportunities for USDA to support America's farmers and ranchers as they build on record agricultural exports. In FY2014, exports of U.S. food and agricultural products reached a record $152.5 billion and supported nearly one million American jobs. The potential for U.S. agricultural exports around the globe is considerable and USDA is taking action to help producers secure and expand market access for American agricultural products. It is also critically important that we have Trade Promotion Authority (TPA) as we seek approval of trade agreements that support and create U.S. jobs while helping American agriculture to compete even more successfully. TPA will help ensure that America's farmers, ranchers, and food processors receive the greatest benefit from these trade agreements, and builds on efforts that have helped achieve record agricultural exports over the past six years.

CONCLUSION

I will say that in regards to agricultural trade with Cuba, that there is potential for expanding U.S. exports over time. It is important to keep in mind that re-establishment of diplomatic relations and opening Embassies is simply the first step of the longer process of normalization relations between the United States and Cuba. It's a complex process, involving bilateral discussions that will continue into the future. The Administration looks forward to engaging with Congress in an honest and serious debate about what we can do to promote positive change in Cuba. Throughout history, agriculture has served as a bridge to foster cooperation, understanding, and the exchange of ideas among people. I have no doubt that agriculture will have an important role to play as these conversations continue and we expand our relationship with the Cuban people in the coming years.

In: Agricultural Trade Between the U.S. and Cuba ISBN: 978-1-63484-430-7
Editor: Lana Valdez

Chapter 5

STATEMENT OF MICHAEL S. BORMAN, DEPUTY ASSISTANT SECRETARY OF COMMERCE FOR EXPORT ADMINISTRATION. HEARING ON "OPPORTUNITIES AND CHALLENGES FOR AGRICULTURE TRADE WITH CUBA"*

Mr. Chairman, Ranking Member Stabenow, Members of the Committee:

Thank you for the opportunity to appear before the Committee today to address the role of the Department of Commerce with regard to regulating agricultural trade with Cuba. As you know, on December 17, 2014, the President announced the most significant changes in Cuba policy in more than fifty years. As he noted, these changes are intended to create more opportunities for the American and Cuban people by increasing commerce, travel, and the free flow of information. To implement these changes, the Department of Commerce's Bureau of Industry and Security (BIS) amended the Export Administration Regulations (EAR) on January 16, 2015, to expand the authorization for exports and re-exports of certain categories of items to Cuba.

The January 16, 2015 amendment of the EAR created License Exception Support for the Cuban People (SCP) and expands the scope of License

* This is an edited, reformatted and augmented version of a statement presented April 21, 2015 before the Senate Committee on Agriculture, Nutrition and Forestry.

Exception Gift Parcels and Humanitarian Donations (GFT). License Exceptions facilitate trade by authorizing specified exports without individual licenses as long as the terms of the exception are followed. License Exception SCP authorizes the export of certain categories of items including building materials such as lumber, plywood, and other wood products for use by the private sector for the construction or renovation of privately-owned buildings, and tools and equipment for private sector agricultural activity. It also authorizes exports of tools, equipment, and supplies to private sector entrepreneurs, including restaurateurs and other food service providers. License Exception GFT now authorizes consolidated shipments of multiple gift parcels, which may contain an unlimited quantity/dollar value of food. Individuals who wish to send food in gift parcels no longer have to search for a party that has received a license from BIS authorizing consolidated shipments to Cuba.

Other provisions of the amendment to the EAR facilitate the export of certain telecommunications items intended to improve the free flow of information to, from, and among the Cuban people and items necessary for the environmental protection of U.S. and international air quality, waters and coastlines.

The changes announced by the President did not, however, result in amendment of the EAR with regard to BIS authorization of exports of agricultural commodities. The Trade Sanctions Reform and Export Enhancement Act (TSRA) of 2000 governs how BIS regulates exports of agricultural commodities. To implement TSRA, BIS created License Exception Agricultural Commodities (AGR) for exports of agricultural commodities from the United States to Cuba provided that they are designated as EAR99 (subject to the EAR but not on the Commerce Control List). To be eligible for License Exception AGR, exporters must provide prior notice to BIS through our online application system. BIS and the Department of State's Bureaus of Economic and Business Affairs and Western Hemisphere Affairs review notices on an expedited basis (generally within 12 business days). Consistent with TSRA, this expedited review process includes screening the ultimate consignee to ensure that the recipient does not promote international terrorism and that the transaction does not raise proliferation concerns. Provided that the transaction meets the terms and conditions of License Exception AGR, exporters may proceed with the transaction once BIS confirms that neither reviewing agency has raised an objection. Exports of agricultural commodities must be made pursuant to a written contract and must take place within one year of the signing of a contract unless the export is a commercial sample or donation (in which case the contract requirement does not apply).

During 2014, BIS processed 56 AGR notifications, valued at $2.4 billion, with an average turnaround of 10 days. Multiple shipments may be made pursuant to a single notification. The dollar value reflects proposed exports, not actual exports. During 2014, exporters made 600 shipments of agricultural products to Cuba. Commerce's Census Bureau reports the value of agriculture exports in calendar year 2014 at about $287 million.

In Cuba, only state-run companies are authorized to engage in foreign trade transactions, and often a whole category of commodities imported from the United States is channeled through a specific company. Shipments of agricultural commodities (specifically food) made under License Exception AGR are generally consigned to ALIMPORT (Empresa Cubana Importadora de Alimentos), a state-run company with the Cuban Ministry of Foreign Trade as its largest shareholder.

The President's announcement did result in new regulatory guidance issued by the Department of the Treasury pursuant to the Cuban Assets Control Regulations regarding "cash in advance" as it pertains to the export of agricultural commodities. My colleague from Treasury's Office of Foreign Assets Control will discuss the regulatory reinterpretation of "cash in advance."

Thank you, once again, for the opportunity to appear before the Committee today. I would be pleased to answer any questions Members may have.

In: Agricultural Trade Between the U.S. and Cuba ISBN: 978-1-63484-430-7
Editor: Lana Valdez

Chapter 6

TESTIMONY OF JOHN E. SMITH, ACTING DIRECTOR, OFFICE OF FOREIGN ASSETS CONTROL, U.S. DEPARTMENT OF THE TREASURY. HEARING ON "OPPORTUNITIES AND CHALLENGES FOR AGRICULTURE TRADE WITH CUBA"*

Good morning, Chairman Roberts, Ranking Member Stabenow, and distinguished members of the committee. Thank you for the invitation to appear before you today to discuss our recent amendments to the Cuban Assets Control Regulations and the implications for agricultural trade with Cuba. I will be addressing the key regulatory amendments made by Treasury's Office of Foreign Assets Control (OFAC) to implement the changes to U.S. policy toward Cuba announced by the President, as well as the restrictions that remain in place. The recent changes are intended to create opportunities for increased agricultural exports to Cuba, among other benefits to U.S. businesses. These regulatory changes ease Cuba sanctions within the continuing constraints of the embargo while advancing the Administration's policy to further engage and empower the Cuban people in their efforts to build a democratic, prosperous, and stable Cuba.

* This is an edited, reformatted and augmented version of testimony presented April 21, 2015 before the Senate Committee on Agriculture, Nutrition and Forestry.

CONTEXT FOR CHANGE

On December 17, the President announced a number of significant policy changes regarding our relationship with Cuba. To implement the sanctions policy changes, OFAC amended the Cuban Assets Control Regulations, and our colleagues at the Department of Commerce amended the Export Administration Regulations (EAR), on January 16. These amendments ease sanctions related to Cuba in a number of key areas, including trade, financial services, travel, and remittances. These changes are intended to have a direct and positive impact on the lives of the Cuban people. They are also aimed at enhancing both commerce and communications between the United States and Cuba, and helping the Cuban people to freely determine their own future.

TRADE THAT BENEFITS AMERICANS AND CUBANS

The President's policy announcement highlighted the need to advance political and economic freedom in Cuba through enhanced commerce and trade between the United States and Cuba. OFAC and the Commerce Department's Bureau of Industry and Security ("BIS") authorize agricultural exports to Cuba, consistent with the provisions of the Trade Sanctions Reform and Export Enhancement Act (TSRA) of 2000, and American farmers, particularly those in the southeastern United States, have been capitalizing on this authorization to export meat and poultry, soybeans, and canned goods, among other items, to Cuba. The recent regulatory changes should ease the export process, thereby facilitating increased U.S. agricultural and other authorized exports to Cuba, benefitting American farmers and approximately 11 million potential Cuban consumers.

OFAC expects the recent rule changes will benefit American exporters in at least four key respects. First, OFAC expanded the financing provisions of the regulations to allow America's agricultural exporters to be more competitive in selling their wares to Cuba. Second, OFAC broadened the ability of U.S. financial institutions to provide services and effectuate payments for exporters and others authorized to engage in trade with Cuba. Third, OFAC authorized trade delegations and exporters satisfying the conditions of its regulations to travel to Cuba – without needing to come to OFAC to apply for and receive a license – and expanded the ability of airlines and other U.S. travel service companies to offer more reliable and potentially cheaper travel services with far less paperwork. Finally, OFAC permitted certain humanitarian projects in Cuba, including those related to agricultural and rural development that promote independent activity. I will talk about each of these rule changes in more detail.

FACILITATING TRADE THROUGH REGULATORY CHANGE

With respect to the first change, OFAC modified the regulatory interpretation of the term "cash in advance," which describes a financing requirement for agricultural trade between the United States and Cuba that is imposed by statute. This term dictates when authorized U.S. exporters to Cuba must receive payment for their goods. Previously, OFAC had interpreted that statutory term to mean that the U.S. exporter had to receive payment from the Cuban importer prior to the goods leaving U.S. shores – an interpretation that American exporters said made their products less competitive than those from other countries. OFAC has now revised its interpretation of the term to mean that payment from the Cuban purchaser is required prior to transfer of title to and control of the goods. This change should provide a more efficient, less expensive means for Cuban importers to purchase American-produced agricultural, medical, and other authorized products. This, in turn, should increase authorized U.S. agricultural and food exports to Cuba, which totaled $360 million last year. Since Cuba imports approximately 80 percent of its food, according to the World Food Program, there is a sizable market available for U.S. businesses to cultivate. U.S. exporters, however, continue to face barriers, including that all U.S. agricultural goods are imported via ALIMPORT (Empresa Cubana Importadora de Alimentos), a Cuban state-run monopoly. Also, U.S. exporters continue to be prevented by statute from offering financing inducements, such as loans, for authorized agricultural exports, a limitation that may prevent them from being as attractive to Cuban importers as third-country competitors.

INCREASING ACCESS TO FINANCIAL SERVICES

With respect to the second key regulatory change, to improve the speed, efficiency, and oversight of authorized payments between the United States and Cuba, OFAC has authorized U.S. banks to establish correspondent accounts at financial institutions in Cuba. This change is intended to ease the flow of authorized payments and eliminate the need for third-country payment structures, which should benefit U.S. exporters to Cuba. Also, travelers to Cuba are now authorized to use their credit and debit cards there, a change which is intended to ease the flow of authorized payments and facilitate authorized travel. These changes will support those individuals and businesses engaged in authorized agricultural and other trade with Cuba by facilitating authorized financial transactions.

Easing Travel Restrictions

With respect to the third key regulatory change, it is important to note that OFAC's Cuba sanctions program is the only such program that restricts travel to a country. The recent changes to the Cuba travel rules build on modifications previously made in 2009 and 2011. Those earlier changes, which were announced by the Administration and implemented by OFAC, eased travel restrictions with respect to Americans' ability to visit family and engage in educational, cultural, journalistic, and religious activities, as well as to engage in certain travel to support licensed exports to Cuba.

The recent regulatory amendments ease travel restrictions further by generally licensing certain additional travel within the 12 existing categories of travel in OFAC's regulations, without the need for a specific license from OFAC. This means that travelers who satisfy the criteria of the general licenses set forth in OFAC's regulations may travel to Cuba and conduct travel-related transactions there without requesting individual authorization from OFAC. The 12 categories of travel are those referenced by Congress in TSRA. Travel to Cuba for tourist activities, which the TSRA statute defines as any activity outside of these 12 categories, remains prohibited.

These 12 categories of authorized travel are:

1) family visits;
2) official business of the U.S. government, foreign governments, and certain intergovernmental organizations;
3) journalistic activity;
4) professional research and professional meetings;
5) educational activities;
6) religious activities;

7) public performances, clinics, workshops, athletic and other competitions, and exhibitions;
8) support for the Cuban people;
9) humanitarian projects;
10) activities of private foundations or research or educational institutes;
11) exportation, importation, or transmission of information or information materials; and
12) certain authorized export transactions.

While certain previous general licenses authorized some travel within the 12 categories of travel, the additional and expanded general licenses that recently took effect are intended to lessen the burden on authorized travelers, making it easier for Americans to interact with the Cuban people, and for trade delegations and authorized exporters to travel to Cuba to promote their products. Specifically, OFAC has issued new general licenses and expanded existing authorizations for travel-related transactions and other transactions incident to the exportation to Cuba of authorized goods, such as agricultural products, for the conduct of market research, commercial marketing, sales negotiation, accompanied delivery or servicing in Cuba of items consistent with the Commerce Department's licensing policy. OFAC's general license authorizing professionals in the agricultural and other sectors to engage in professional meetings in Cuba, provided certain conditions are satisfied, will also support U.S. exporters in coordinating with their Cuban counterparts.

The recent regulatory amendments also authorize U.S. airlines to provide air carrier services to, from, and within Cuba in connection with authorized travel. Air carriers wishing to provide these services still need to secure regulatory approvals from other concerned U.S. Government agencies, including the Departments of Transportation and Homeland Security. Persons subject to U.S. jurisdiction, such as travel agents and tour group operators, also may now provide travel services in connection with authorized travel. These changes are intended to make authorized travel easier and less expensive by reducing the paperwork burden for, and increasing competition among, those providing travel and air carrier services.

Increasing Access to Remittances

With respect to the fourth key regulatory change, and to help strengthen Cuban civil society, OFAC eased certain restrictions on remittances to Cuba, following similar actions taken in 2009 and 2011. In the recent amendments, OFAC increased that quarterly limitation on non-family remittances from $500 to $2,000 per person per quarter. OFAC also generally authorized remittances to certain individuals and independent non-governmental organizations in Cuba for humanitarian projects, including those related to agricultural and rural development, support for the Cuban people, and the development of private businesses in Cuba, with no limitation on the amount. These changes are intended to facilitate the flow of authorized funds directly to the Cuban people. This increased access to funds should significantly benefit the Cuban people, as remittances are one of the primary sources of income for many Cubans. Increased remittances will afford individual Cubans with increased financial resources with which to purchase American-produced agricultural goods and develop more private economic activity.

TELECOMMUNICATIONS AND THE FREE FLOW OF INFORMATION

Another key area of regulatory change is telecommunications. Cuba has an Internet penetration of approximately five percent – one of the lowest in the world. Coupled with the exorbitant costs of both personal telecommunications devices and Internet access, this has severely limited the ability of Cubans to communicate with each other and the outside world. In order to better facilitate the free flow of information to, from, and among the Cuban people, in accordance with the President's announcement, OFAC eased restrictions to better provide efficient and adequate telecommunications services between the United States and Cuba and to increase access to telecommunications and Internet-based services for the Cuban people. Among other things, these changes should support Cubans in increasing their knowledge of the United States, its democratic traditions, and the quality and availability of U.S. exports, and help American exporters better connect with more potential Cuban consumers.

OBSERVATION

We expect that it will take some time for the impact of the recent regulatory changes to take effect, both among the private sector and the public more broadly, and the impact will be somewhat dependent on the Government of Cuba and its receptiveness to these changes. OFAC has made all of the regulatory changes necessary to implement the policy changes announced by the President in December, and we are now focusing our efforts on facilitating and clarifying the implementation of these regulatory changes. To assist with this, OFAC is actively engaged in regular outreach to help the public and private sector better understand the changes, and how best to avail themselves of the benefits of these changes. Specifically, OFAC has addressed queries from and provided briefings to trade groups as well as the Chamber of Commerce, and a number of Industry Trade Advisory Committees (ITAC) under the auspices of the Department of Commerce and the Office of the U.S. Trade Representative, among others. Also, OFAC has published a number of Frequently Asked Questions (FAQs) on its website to address questions regarding the implications of the recent regulatory amendments. OFAC will be issuing additional FAQs to provide further clarification as needed.

CONCLUSION

In conclusion, I should make one point absolutely clear: Even with these changes I've described, most transactions between the United States and Cuba – including most export, import, and other activities – remain prohibited. As OFAC implements these recent changes, we will continue to enforce the Cuba sanctions program vigorously and take actions against violators, as appropriate.

The President's December 17 announcement laid out a new course for our relations with Cuba, driven by a hope for a more positive future for the Cuban people. OFAC's regulatory amendments to the Cuban Assets Control Regulations, in concert with the regulatory revisions my colleague at Commerce will highlight, mark significant changes to our Cuba sanctions that implement the new policy announced by the President. These changes are intended to directly benefit the Cuban people and help them to freely determine their own future, as well as to support U.S. businesses and American exporters to Cuba.

Thank you. I welcome your questions.

In: Agricultural Trade Between the U.S. and Cuba ISBN: 978-1-63484-430-7
Editor: Lana Valdez

Chapter 7

TESTIMONY OF MICHAEL V. BEALL, PRESIDENT & CEO, NATIONAL COOPERATIVE BUSINESS ASSOCIATION. HEARING ON "OPPORTUNITIES AND CHALLENGES FOR AGRICULTURE TRADE WITH CUBA"*

Chairman Roberts, Ranking Member Stabenow, and Members of the Committee,

My name is Michael Beall, I am President and CEO of NCBA CLUSA. NCBA CLUSA is the apex trade association for cooperative business in the United States and an international development organization. Our work provides cross-sector education, support, and advocacy that helps cooperatives thrive. We also engage with cooperative sectors around the world, including Cuba.

It is an honor to be here to discuss new ways forward in U.S. Cuba relations; notably through trade. I think you will find my testimony today will take a slightly different track than other panels as our organization recently has already been highly focused on cooperative development inside Cuba as a result of changes to laws within that country.

* This is an edited, reformatted and augmented version of testimony presented April 21, 2015 before the Senate Committee on Agriculture, Nutrition and Forestry.

Let me start today by thanking Chairman Roberts for holding today's hearing and the Committee for recognizing that the recent regulatory changes impacting U.S. Cuba relations have led to a great number of difficult questions and political challenges but also provide for great opportunities. If I am to leave you with two important thoughts today it is that first, the United States should view Cuban cooperatives as key actors in building economic ties to that country and providing the Cuban people with economic independence from the state through cooperative business (or member) ownership; and second, that U.S. cooperatives are well-positioned and eager to play a role in trade and private sector development in Cuba.

In the United States, member-owned cooperatives are a vibrant and viable alternative form of business and part of a strong U.S. economy, and have been since the early 19th century. Consumers, producers, and workers throughout America and other parts of the world continue to seek the economic freedoms and choices that cooperative businesses provide in virtually every sector of the economy. When consumers anywhere in the world choose cooperative businesses to provide for their needs, they are choosing a business model that not only provides high quality, low cost options, but also one that supports the cooperative values of self-help, democracy, and concern for community.

Cooperatives (or co-ops for short) are owned and controlled by their members; the people who use its services or buy its goods. Cooperatives use any profits earned by their business for the benefit of their members, either by reinvesting in their business, lowering prices or interest rates, or by returning dividends to members.

Most equity comes from the member-owners and not from outside investors, which makes cooperatives a distinct alternative business model. Cooperatives are characterized by the fact that they are formed to serve their members and not solely to earn a profit. Among key principles, cooperatives are democratically governed. Every member gets an equal vote in determining a cooperative's governance.

In many ways, cooperatives resemble other businesses. They have similar physical facilities, perform similar functions, and follow sound business practices. They are usually incorporated under state law and operate under the direction of a board of directors with bylaws.

Because of their unique structure and composition, cooperatives often are misunderstood and face hurdles when interacting in the marketplace and with governments. NCBA CLUSA's work provides cross-sector education, support, and advocacy that helps cooperatives thrive here and abroad.

American consumers come into contact with cooperative business every day in virtually every sector of the economy; from agriculture, childcare, credit unions, energy, insurance, food, healthcare, housing, retail, and the media and telecommunications. According to federally supported research on cooperative businesses by the University of Wisconsin Center on Cooperatives, we know that:

- Approximately 29,000 cooperatives are in operation today
- They sustain 2 million jobs annually
- Contribute $652 billion in annual sales
- Generate $150 billion in income
- Possess $3 trillion in assets
- 1 in 3 Americans are members of a co-op and collectively hold 350 million memberships nationwide
- 92 million Americans turn to 7,500 credit unions for their financial services
- Most of the nation's 2 million farmers are farmer co-op members and provide 250,000 jobs and $8 billion in annual wages
- 42 million Americans rely on electricity from 900 rural electric co-ops in 47 states – making up 42% of the nation's electric distribution and covering 75% of the nation
- 233 million people are served by co-op owned and affiliated insurance companies
- 1.2 million rural Americans are served by the 260 telephone cooperatives in 31 states
- 50,000 American families rely on cooperative daycare and preschools for the care of their children.

We know that the cooperative model is a powerful tool in developing countries as well. Worldwide, over a billion people belong to a cooperative.

Along with the U.S., capitalistic countries around the world view cooperatives as a viable business model; in Cuba, cooperatives are now being prioritized in the development of the country's nascent private sector. Since early 2013, Cuba has been working to shift its economy from state-controlled enterprises to citizen-controlled and owned cooperatives; this shift is a key strategy to lessening state control and strengthening market-based approaches to the economy.

As in the U.S., cooperatives in Cuba perform vital business functions. Historically in Cuba, cooperatives were primarily found in the agricultural sector. There is a 50 year history of agricultural cooperatives in Cuba that date back prior to the revolution. There are nearly 5,200 agriculture cooperatives currently operating in Cuba that contribute 80% of all fruits and vegetables consumed in Cuba. Given new guidelines for the economy established by the Cuban government in 2011, that situation is changing dramatically with the emergence of non-agricultural cooperatives (NAC) in numerous economic activities. Of the three types of agricultural cooperatives previously established, at least two of them should be considered "private enterprise" under the strictest of definitions. They, along with the NACs, are briefly described below.

In the Cuban legal conceptual framework, cooperatives are private entities jointly owned by a group of associates as defined and protected under their laws. This attribute distinguishes this sector from the other types of enterprise which are state-owned, private (individual ownership), or joint ventures (Cuban state and foreigners). In Cuba there is a fundamental demarcation between state and non-state businesses. Cooperatives of all forms are non-state entities, though they may have varying commercial and financial connections with the state.

Cuban cooperatives in general, but especially the newest ones emerging, face many technical and educational challenges with regard to how to operate most effectively as strong associations and businesses. International exchanges with cooperative groups like NCBA CLUSA and our member cooperatives will provide valuable learning tools, best practices, and exchanges that can help strengthen this sector and its role in privatizing the economy.

Brief Description of Cuban Cooperative Forms

Agricultural Cooperatives

Cooperativas de Créditos y Servicios (CCS)/Credit and Service Cooperatives

Farmers with small amounts of land first formed them in the early 1960s. CCS cooperative members are private landowners who hold their land separately but join together to obtain and utilize agricultural credits and services. According to official statistics, as of 2010, CCS cooperatives have a total membership of 362,440 farmers that own 35.2% of cultivable land.

Cooperativas de Producción Agropecuaria (CPA)/Agricultural Production Cooperatives

CPAs were formed in the mid-1970s by small private landowners joining together much like those in CCS cooperatives. However in the CPA structure, members contribute their land to participate in joint land ownership with the other members. The land remains totally private but mutually owned by members. According to official statistics, as of 2010, there were a total of 30,000 members owning 8.8% of cultivable land.

Unidad Básica de Producción Cooperativa (UBPC)/Basic Units of Cooperative Production

UBPCs emerged in the early 1990s as a means for the state to break up large state farms. Workers own their production, make management decisions, and operate as cooperatives, but do not own their land. They have usufruct from the State, which retains ownership of the properties. According to official records, as of 2010, UBPCs have a total membership of 187,000, and work 30.9% of cultivable land.

Non-Agricultural Cooperatives (NAC)

Historically, Cuba has not had enabling laws for the formation of NAC cooperatives. Law No. 305 establishing their legal structure was enacted in November 2012. NACs are not state enterprises.

Article 2, Section 2 of their Law states, "A cooperative has its own juridical and patrimonial persona; it may use, enjoy, and dispose of the assets of its property; cover its own expenses with its income; and meet its obligations from its own patrimony." Article 4 of the same law lists seven cooperative values that shall guide the behavior of the entities including their voluntary nature, internal democracy, and community responsibility among others. These aggregate values are strikingly similar to those voted on and promulgated by the worldwide membership of the International Cooperative Alliance.

Currently NACs represent a tiny fraction of the Cuban workforce, about 350 have formed, which is less than .4% of their economy. However, based on official government statements and policy priorities, that number could expand to 15% - 20% of employment in the coming years.

NACs originate in two ways. There is a legally defined process for the creation of "grassroots" or "bottoms up" cooperatives in which a minimum of 3 people agree to form a joint enterprise within the framework of the regulations. These cooperative members jointly are the owners of all aspects of their business. Most common to date, however, has been the practice of offering state enterprise employees the option of forming a cooperative or likely face the closure of the enterprise. In such a conversion from state enterprise to cooperative, all the norms and regulations guiding performance are in place regarding management, internal functioning, control of production, etc. However the land and buildings remain state property and are leased to the cooperative.

Based on these changes, in early 2014, NCBA CLUSA established the U.S. Cuba Cooperative Working Group (USCCWG) to explore opportunities to engage with Cuba on cooperative development and released a Cuba Research Trip report on its initial findings. I would like to include in my testimony today a copy of that report as well as an outline and scope of work of the USCCWG.

We remain optimistic that these internal changes in Cuba, coupled with the recent U.S. regulatory changes, will create enhanced opportunities to help Cuban workers improve their living standards, gain greater business ownership, and economic independence from the state. This is the mission and objective of the USCCWG.

Cubans have been able to form cooperatives in non-agricultural sectors only since July 2013, so most of the immediate opportunity for trade is in agriculture. The country's non-agricultural cooperatives are currently aimed at meeting local needs. The Cuban government is emphasizing this sector because of the need to increase food production. The mutual trade potential is enormous, but in the short run, especially from U.S. cooperatives to Cuban cooperatives. I think the need for inputs, for equipment, and for know-how are large. I think the cooperative sector here in the U.S. is very well positioned to do that.

The question about trade is important in that as markets start to open up, hopefully these cooperatives will have better access to raw materials — commodities such as seeds and fertilizers that will help them to continue to grow their businesses.

Cuban cooperatives eventually might be able to export certain crops to the U.S., particularly those that are more tropically oriented; such as fruits, coffee, or sugar. The Cuban government is currently analyzing how the cooperatives operate in order to develop a definitive law in 2016 that will improve the commercial environment for them.

What would NCBA CLUSA view as a positive outcome for expanded U.S./Cuban cooperative relations? A great deal depends on how the new regulatory changes take shape in addition to the existing embargo restrictions and how much the Cuban government will allow for change. Much is out of our control both politically here in the United States as well as in Cuba and challenges with capabilities by the Cuban government. However, we would like to see positive enabling environments in which cooperatives can thrive and which protect the economic freedoms and choices of people in Cuba. We hold that United States government policy needs to continue to provide recognition of cooperatives as supporting the nascent Cuban private sector as well as parity for cooperatives equal to other forms of business interested in Cuba's economic transition.

We were pleased to see the Commerce Department recently update its Export Administration Regulations (15 CFR Parts 736, 740, 746, 748; https://www.federalregister.gov/articles/2015/01/16/2015-00590/cuba-provi ding-support-for-thecuban-people) and add a new license exception to enable exports to empower the nascent Cuban private sector by supporting private economic activity. Exports providing building materials; goods for entrepreneurs such as mechanics, hairstylists, and restauranteurs; and tools and equipment for agriculture activity, many which are non-agricultural cooperatives, now have a license exemption. This is intended to facilitate lower-priced access to goods to improve living standards and gain greater economic independence from the state. Prior to this rule, these activities required a license to support the embargo.

I would like to include in my testimony today, copies of letters that NCBA CLUSA sent to Secretary Jack Lew at the U.S. Department of Treasury and to Secretary Penny Pritzker at the U.S. Department of Commerce, outlining our views on recent regulatory changes announced by their Departments.

Cooperative development and growth in Cuba can be a positive development toward advancing the needs of the Cuban people as well as meeting the objectives of the U.S. government to support the strengthening of the Cuban private sector and greater independence from the State. Much work remains to be done. We look forward to the continued work of our U.S. Cuba Cooperative Working Group, and to fostering expanded engagement with the Cuban cooperative sector. This will allow both cooperative sectors to exchange important information, deepen economic ties, and provide a platform for additional support and technical assistance. NCBA CLUSA stands ready as a resource and convener of the U.S. cooperative sector to work with all levels in the U.S. government in this pivotal moment for U.S. Cuba relations.

Thank you again for allowing me to testify before you today.

In: Agricultural Trade Between the U.S. and Cuba ISBN: 978-1-63484-430-7
Editor: Lana Valdez

Chapter 8

STATEMENT OF TERRY HARRIS, SENIOR VICE PRESIDENT, MARKETING AND RISK MANAGEMENT, RICELAND FOODS. HEARING ON "OPPORTUNITIES AND CHALLENGES FOR AGRICULTURE TRADE WITH CUBA"*

Thank you, Mr. Chairman. I am Terry Harris, senior vice president of marketing and risk management at Riceland Foods, headquartered in Stuttgart, Arkansas. I appreciate this opportunity to appear before the Committee on behalf of Riceland Foods and the USA Rice Federation.

Riceland is a family-farmer owned cooperative formed in 1921 to market rice. Today, Riceland serves approximately 6,000 farmer-members in Arkansas and Missouri who grow rice, soybeans and wheat. The cooperative markets about a third of the rice grown in the southern United States and about a fourth of the national production.

Riceland is primarily a direct exporter, selling directly to buyers in importing countries, although we sometimes sell rice through other U.S. export firms and international shippers for delivery to importing countries. As a result of this direct approach, our staff is well schooled in the details of everyday management of logistics and finance related to the export business.

---

* This is an edited, reformatted and augmented version of a statement presented April 21, 2015 before the Senate Committee on Agriculture, Nutrition and Forestry.

Riceland Foods is proud to be a member of the USA Rice Federation. USA Rice represents all segments of the U.S. rice industry. Rice is grown in seven states including Arkansas, California, Louisiana, Texas, Mississippi, Missouri and Florida. Nearly half of the U.S. crop is grown in eastern Arkansas. The industry markets rice in all 50 states and to 125 countries worldwide. USA Rice is a founding member of the U.S. Agricultural Coalition for Cuba, a broad-based group of U.S. agricultural and food organizations seeking to re-establish Cuba as a market for U.S. food and agriculture exports.

My objective today is to discuss the past and potential trade relationship between the U.S. rice industry and Cuba, a future that I believe holds great promise for U.S. rice farmers and U.S. agriculture.

The United States exports half of the rice produced annually, so maintaining existing markets, as well as developing new markets, are key components to the industry's success.

Our largest export markets include Canada, Mexico and Central America. Securing additional export markets is important to the economies in rice growing states. Therefore, the U.S. rice industry wholeheartedly supports the opportunity to move to normal commercial relations with Cuba.

Prior to the U.S. embargo on Cuba more than 50 years ago, the island was the number one export destination for U.S. rice. Annual rice shipments reached as much as a quarter of a million metric tons in the 1950s, and the U.S. accounted for more than half of Cuba's rice imports.

Prospects brightened with passage of the Trade Sanctions Reform and Export Enhancement Act of 2000, when U.S. agriculture and food exports to Cuba were granted, or what many of us believed at the time to be, a broad exemption from the embargo.

In November 2001, I had the opportunity to make the first sale of U.S. rice to Cuba since the embargo was imposed. It was an incredibly intense and interesting negotiation as we developed contract terms and quality specifications for a country which, at that time, had not purchased goods from the U.S. in 40 years.

I found the leadership of the Cuban buying organization informed, shrewd, and very professional. I also was in Cuba to witness the first shipment of U.S. rice when it arrived in the Port of Havana. It was an incredible experience for me to see how excited they were with the quality of rice they had purchased for the people of Cuba. I saw what can happen when barriers are removed and people are allowed to meet and find common ground for cooperation and trade.

As recently as 2004, sales of U.S. rice to Cuba were valued at $64 million.

The success of rice and other U.S. agriculture products in Cuba was seriously curtailed in large part following a change by the Office of Foreign Assets Control in the definition of "payment of cash in advance" in 2005. U.S. rice exports to Cuba dropped to zero following this regulatory change.

Cuba is a significant market for rice, importing about $300 million worth of rice annually, with a per capita consumption of 177 pounds per person. By contrast, per capita U.S. consumption is less than 30 pounds. Currently, most of Cuba's rice imports come from Vietnam.

With the port of New Orleans located less than 700 miles from Havana, the U.S. is in a better position to serve the rice needs of the Cuban people in terms of required transit time and the cost of freight.

With the lifting of the embargo and the restoration of trade and travel with Cuba, we estimate that the U.S. could regain 20 to 30 percent of the Cuban rice business within two years, or an estimated 90,000 to 135,000 metric tons of new demand for U.S. rice farmers based on USDA's current estimate of overall annual Cuban import demand. We would anticipate the U.S. share of the market would exceed 50 percent within five years and could reach 75 percent or more within 10 years.

On January 15, 2015, OFAC made changes to the regulations on trade with Cuba that allowed for the definition of "payment of cash in advance" to revert to the pre-2005 wording. We applaud this measure, as well as other actions by the Obama administration to facilitate trade. However, there are still obstacles to conducting normal trade with Cuba.

I stated earlier that we are seeking normal commercial relations with Cuba. This means allowing U.S. citizens to travel and spend money in Cuba without restrictions as well as allowing Cuba to export their goods to the United States as they do to most countries around the world so they will gain the resources and increased demand to import U.S. food and agricultural products. It also means permitting the full range of commercial banking and financial relationships to facilitate trade based on individual exporter assessments of the risk of doing business in Cuba.

With the lifting of the embargo and the restoration of trade and travel, normal commercial relations would be restored. This would allow direct banking and extending of credit under commercial terms which would position the U.S. to compete with Vietnam for the Cuban rice market.

The U.S. rice industry and Riceland Foods is committed to building the Cuba market for our product. Our company has made numerous trips to Cuba to meet with Cuba's national importer of rice and food products. USA Rice has spent just under $900,000 in rice industry promotion funds since 2003 to promote the high quality and efficiency of U.S. rice in the Cuba market. We intend to continue these activities.

To give U.S. rice the chance to compete in Cuba, the rice industry seeks the ultimate lifting of the embargo and the elimination of all restrictions on tourism and trade with Cuba. This, of course, requires Congressional action.

Thank you for the opportunity to share our views with the Committee. I would be pleased to respond to any questions.

In: Agricultural Trade Between the U.S. and Cuba ISBN: 978-1-63484-430-7
Editor: Lana Valdez

Chapter 9

TESTIMONY OF C. PARR ROSSON III, PROFESSOR & DEPARTMENT HEAD, DEPARTMENT OF AGRICULTURE ECONOMICS, TEXAS A&M UNIVERSITY. HEARING ON "OPPORTUNITIES AND CHALLENGES FOR AGRICULTURE TRADE WITH CUBA"*

Mr. Chairman and esteemed members of the Committee, I thank you for the opportunity to testify on the opportunities and challenges for agricultural trade with Cuba. I am Parr Rosson, Professor and Department Head in the Agricultural Economics Department at Texas A&M University. I have been at Texas A&M since 1989. From 1997 and until becoming Department Head in 2012, I was the Director of the Center for North American Studies (CNAS) at Texas A&M. I have been involved in research and extension education related to Cuba for 15 years. In that capacity, I conducted dozens of economic impact analyses examining how increasing U.S. food and agricultural exports to Cuba will impact the U.S. economy and the economies of the states that produce those goods for export. During 2010 as the House Agriculture Committee was considering HR 4645, we conducted 16 analyses at Committee staff request describing how the relaxation of travel restrictions and financing regulations

* This is an edited, reformatted and augmented version of testimony presented April 21, 2015 before the Senate Committee on Agriculture, Nutrition and Forestry.

would increase U.S. exports and stimulate business activity and job growth throughout the U.S. economy. Since then, I have continued to investigate changes in Cuba and how they affect U.S. agriculture. In general, we find that exports create jobs, and exports to Cuba are no exception. For every $73,600 in U.S. food and agricultural exports to Cuba, one job is created in the United States and an additional $170,000 in economic activity is required to support those additional exports.

Opportunities and Market Potential

Cuba has the potential to become a major market for U.S, agricultural exports and to develop into a market that is quite diverse, with bulk staple products, such as corn, wheat, soybeans and rice, being important in the near term. But, over time as the market grows, and the tastes and preferences of the average Cuban become more sophisticated, U.S. exports will be well positioned to capture a growing share of the high-value food market. So as to not overemphasize the present size of the Cuban market, U.S. exports to Cuba of $286 million represented less than one percent of total U.S. agricultural exports of $169 billion in 2014.

Our previous research indicates that U.S. export potential could exceed the record $709 million set in 2008. With a more open economy, less regulation by both governments, strong tourism and remittances, U.S. food and agricultural exports have the potential to exceed $1.2 billion annually within five years (Rosson, Adcock and Manthei). While much of this additional export volume may be consumed by international visitors, a growing share will also make its way into the Cuban populace, spurring additional demand for U.S. products.

In 2014, U.S. exports to Cuba were $286 million, supported $867 million in total business activity and provided employment for 3,885 workers throughout the U.S. economy. U.S. agriculture receives economic gains from increased agricultural exports, with benefits accruing to non-agricultural sectors such as business and financial services, real estate, wholesale and retail trade and health care. Approximately 45 percent of the gains in business activity go to non-agricultural sectors, while the majority of gains, 55 percent, go to agricultural producers, agribusinesses and related firms.

These most recent exports have been concentrated in poultry, the soybean complex and corn. Major exports included frozen leg quarters and other poultry ($148 million), soybeans and soybean meal ($98 million) and corn ($28 million). Together these three product categories represented 96 percent of U.S.

agricultural exports to Cuba in 2014. Other U.S. exports were feeds/fodders ($9.4 million), dairy products ($1.4 million), pork ($1.3 million) and fresh fruit, prepared and snack foods ($379,000). U.S. poultry claimed 73 percent of the poultry market in Cuba, while the soy complex represented 20 percent and corn one-half of the market. Cuba is now the seventh largest market for U.S. exports in the Caribbean/Central American region, but has potential to become more important.

Cuba is a centrally-planned economy located 90 miles south of Key West, Florida. The proximity to the United States makes Cuba economically, socially and politically important. Since the U.S. embargo was implemented in 1962, effectively severing diplomatic and economic relations, U.S. firms have been prohibited from doing business there.

Nearly three-fourths of the labor force is employed by the government of Cuba (GOC) at a wage of approximately $20/month. The literacy rate is estimated at 99.8 percent, the highest in the Western Hemisphere (CIA). The GOC, however, is involved in virtually every aspect of the business and personal lives of its citizens. Trade and investment are strictly limited and controlled by government regulation. Further, food and agricultural imports are required to enter the country through Empresa Comercializadora de Alimentos (ALIMPORT).

International trade between the United States and Cuba is strictly regulated by both governments. U.S. firms may export foods, agricultural good and medicines to Cuba. Recent regulatory changes allow the importation of selected Cuban products, but these products must be purchased from private businesses, not the Cuban government. So, while some relaxation of regulation has occurred, there are significant regulatory impediments to trade in food and agricultural products.

However, a combination of factors led to the growth of U.S. food and agricultural exports to Cuba during the early 2000s. First, passage of the Trade Sanctions Reform and Export Enhancement Act of 2000 allowed U.S. firms to legally export their agricultural products to Cuba and travel there for business purposes. Second, the rapid onset of hurricane Michelle in 2001 led to the destruction of most food crops in Cuba, and subsequently to acute food shortages. This prompted Cuba to begin the importation of U.S. food and agricultural products on a commercial basis for the first time since the embargo was imposed.

From modest beginnings of $141 million in 2002, U.S. exports grew to $398 million in 2004 and peaked at $709 million in 2008. U.S. exports then fell to $460 million in 2012, $350 million in 2013 and $286 million in 2014

(Figure 1). For January and February, 2015 U.S. exports to Cuba were down 56 percent from the same period last year to $35 million (Foreign Agricultural Service, USDA).

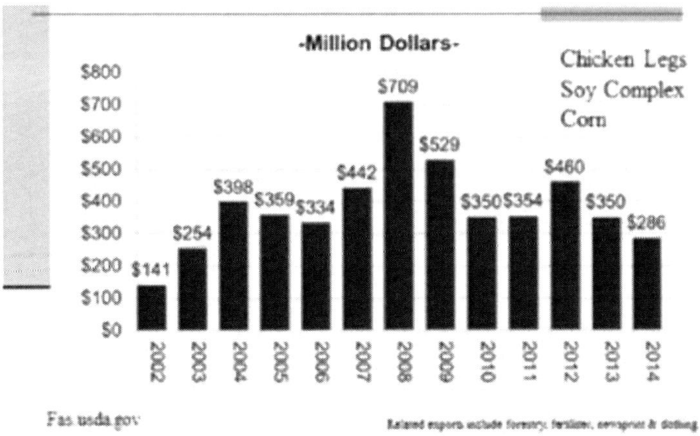

Figure 1. US Food, Ag & Related Exports to Cuba.

This recent export performance is in sharp contrast to 2009, when a much larger and more diverse mix of U.S. products were exported to Cuba. In 2009, U.S. agricultural exports to Cuba of $529 million required 8,588 jobs and generated $1.6 billion in total economic activity. Major U.S. exports were frozen broilers/turkeys and other poultry ($144 million), soybeans and soybean products ($133 million) corn ($120 million), and wheat ($73 million). These four product categories represented 89 percent of total U.S. agricultural exports to Cuba. Other important U.S. exports were animal feeds ($26 million), pork ($11 million), dry beans ($4.3 million), and processed foods and phosphate fertilizers ($3 million) each. Minor exports were apples, pears and grapes ($2.6 million), margarine ($2.2 million), and treated poles ($1.7 million).

There are several reasons for this sharp decline in U.S. exports. First, Cuba has diversified its food suppliers by shifting away from U.S. products in favor of those from Brazil, Canada, Argentina, Mexico, Spain, France, Ukraine, and Vietnam. Credit terms are offered by some of these countries, allowing ALIMPORT to conserve hard currency and use credit to make larger purchases over periods of several months or longer. Sustained high prices for many agricultural commodities and a strong U.S. dollar also negatively impacted U.S. exports over the last several years. Lower earnings from tourism, and nickel exports also hampered the GOC from continuing large cash expenditures on imported food. Perhaps another reason may have been the deliberate decision by the GOC to move away from the United States as a food supplier. After a decade of trying to influence U.S. policy and failing, persistence may have waned. The net result was a loss of U.S. competitiveness and market share, followed by a precipitous 59 percent decline in U.S. exports between 2008 and 2014.

Cuba, however, does have potential for growth as a market for U.S. food and agricultural exports. With a population of 11 million, Cuba is similar in demographic composition and structure to the Dominican Republic, the largest U.S. market in the Caribbean/Central American region. Cuba also mirrors Guatemala, a market that has grown 38 percent since over the past five years.

In 2014, the Dominican Republic had a population of 10 million, with a labor force of 4.9 million. The proportion of the population between the ages of 25-54 was 39 percent. Per capita gross domestic product (GDP) was estimated at $9,200. GDP was composed of 15 percent agricultural production, 22 percent industrial production and 63 percent services (CIA). In 2014, the Dominican Republic imported $1.4 billion from the United States, compared to $1.1 billion in 2010, an average annual growth rate of nearly seven percent.

Cuba, by contrast, had a labor force of 5.2 million in 2010 (CIA). Per capita GDP was estimated to be $10,200. This figure includes adjustment for government subsidized food, housing, transportation and medical care. Agriculture accounted for four percent of GDP, while industrial production was 22 percent and services was 74 percent. The proportion of the population between the ages of 25-54 was 47 percent, higher than the Dominican Republic and positive in terms of U.S. export growth potential since that age group tends to experience the highest levels of expenditure on food and other consumer products. These demographic comparisons give some idea of the potential the Cuban food market could have if it becomes more market oriented, less restricted by government regulation and experiences investment in business and infrastructure.

Currently and likely for the near future, three key factors will influence the volume and mix of U.S. food and agricultural exports to Cuba. First, remittances to Cuba, largely from Cuban-Americans in the United States, represent a major source of income and purchasing power for about 60 percent of Cuban households and an important source of foreign exchange for the GOC.

Cuba's exports are also important for sustaining the economy and the ability to import food. With imports representing a much as 80 percent of food consumption in some years, access to foreign exchange is crucial. Tourism ($1.9 billion), nickel/cobalt ($1.0 billion) and pharmaceuticals ($547 million) were Cuba's three most important exports out of a total of $5.3 billion in 2013. Other major exports included sugar ($449 million), tobacco ($245 million) and rum ($154 million). Cuba's ability to purchase food fluctuates widely as global markets for these products influence prices and volumes traded.

Finally, U.S. export success is heavily influenced by decisions on the part of the GOC and ALIMPORT related to which products to purchase, at what price and in what volumes. As relations between the two countries improve, there is reason to be optimistic that U.S. exports will expand, leading to a more robust and competitive market.

The present product mix of frozen leg quarters, soybean meal and corn could certainly increase to include more processed foods and high value products such as pork, beef, prepared meats such as sausage and hot dogs, along with condiments such as sauces, seasonings, mayonnaise, mustard and other products. Dairy products, rice and wheat also have strong potential in the market. Snack foods, frozen desserts, soups, gelatins and canned fruit and vegetables all have potential. Raisins, nuts, fresh fruit and vegetables, along with gum, bottled water, wine, beer and spirts all have potential. These products were exported to Cuba to some degree until 2012 when the Cuban government began to make substantial food purchases from other suppliers.

CHALLENGES FACING U.S. EXPORTS TO CUBA

There are several constraints that may limit the performance of U.S. exports to Cuba. Consumer incomes, infrastructure/logistics, and policy and regulation are among the most important. Consumer income growth is one of the critical factors affecting market potential in Cuba. With the large majority of the population on fixed, low incomes, consumer disposable incomes are limited. Remittances, largely from Cuban-Americans in the United States are an important component of household income. These funds are transferred directly to Cubans and represent a substantial boost to consumer purchasing power. Estimated to increase eight percent from $2.77 billion in 2013 to $3.0 billion in 2014, remittances are likely to have a substantial positive economic effect on the Cuban economy and U.S. exports, spurring expenditures by those who receive them and fostering additional investment in small business ventures (Cuba Standard). Should remittances decline, however, there would be direct negative impacts on Cuban consumers and followed by lower purchases of U.S. food products.

Tourism is also an important income source for those Cubans who work in restaurants, hotels and other tourist related businesses, such as transportation. With a record 3.0 million visitors in 2014, spending an average of $629/trip, tourism represents a key component of the Cuban economy that generated $1.9 billion last year (Carrillo). Approximately 40 percent of all visitors to Cuba are from Canada, followed by Germany, England, Italy, France and Mexico (ONE). Allowing U.S. visitors to use credit cards will also have a positive economic impact, but the exact amount is uncertain and more research is required.

Cuba also relies on exports of nickel and cobalt, pharmaceuticals, sugar and rum. International market volatility due to wide swings in commodity prices can limit the amount of currency available for food purchases, and certainly dampen U.S. export potential.

Infrastructure and logistics pose special problems for U.S. exporters. Internet access in Cuba is severely limited, with only an estimated five percent of the population having access. While some tourist hotels provide internet access in rooms and terminals in the lobby, many have limited access or none at all. This can hamper U.S. business operations and communications with ALIMPORT officials since some may not have consistent access to email or internet communications. Lack of internet and email can certainly have a negative effect on communications between Cuban officials and U.S. businesses after deals are made and the U.S. representative returns home.

Electrical power, while adequate most of the time, does have limitations. Intermittent outages and complete loss of power are common occurrences. When this occurs, perishable food products located in warehouses, at Cuban Customs, or in groceries or restaurants may be subject to damage, partial spoilage or complete loss. Additional investment in power infrastructure will be an important factor in determining the amount of U.S. perishables that can be imported and retained in storage. Bulk cargoes, such as corn, soybeans, wheat and rice also face constraints due to antiquated unloading facilities at ports, limited vessel size constraints and slow loading capacities. The development of an efficient, reliable supply chain is crucial to future U.S. export success.

Many U.S. competitors in the Cuban market offer some type of credit terms to ALIMORT for food purchases. U.S. firms are precluded from doing so and also face an added constraint of being required to offer only cash-in-advance sales, or cash against documents. U.S. exporters cannot use letters of credit to facilitate sales and manage risk, raising the cost of U.S. products and making them less competitive relative to Spain, Canada, Brazil, China and Vietnam. Reducing the cost and time necessary to process payment for U.S. exports to Cuba would have positive economic impacts in terms of increased exports and economic activity. U.S. exports to Cuba would be expected to rise by $271.2 million/year, requiring an additional $561.9 million in business activity for a total economic impact of $833.1 million and supporting 4,478 new jobs (Rosson, Adcock and Manthei). In summary, consistent, transparent and facilitative policies related to export finance for U.S. exports to Cuba would have positive economic impacts on U.S. exports and the U.S. economy.

BACKGROUND ON AGRICULTURE IN CUBA

Agriculture (including sugar) accounts for 4.2 percent of Cuba gross domestic product (GDP), compared to 18 percent for repairs, 17 percent for public health and manufacturing at 15 percent (ONE). Cuba has a moderate, subtropical climate with an average of 330 days of sunshine annually. The island's weather is characterized by a dry season (November-April) and a rainy season (May-October). The average temperature ranges from 75 degrees in the West to 80 degrees in the East. Humidity averages about 80 percent and average annual rainfall is 52 inches, with about 39 inches falling during the rainy season (Cuba Weather).

Roughly 50 percent of Cuba's land is classified as agricultural, with 75 percent of that land area in relatively flat to gently rolling terrain and suitable for tropical and subtropical agricultural production (USDA). According to the Food and Agriculture Organization of the United Nations, however, about 70 percent of Cuba's arable land has low organic matter content, while 45 percent is characterized by low fertility, 42 percent is eroded and 40 is poorly drained. These soil conditions are attributed to poor land management, including continuous tillage, overgrazing, and inadequate or improper use of irrigation and drainage systems.

Agricultural in Cuba land is evenly distributed between cropland (46 percent) and pasture (54 percent) (USDA). Recently, a large, but so far undocumented, amount of Cuba's cropland was taken out of permanent crop production and placed in native, unimproved pasture. It is suspected that this was done in an attempt to increase milk production, which has declined about 10 percent since 2003. This occurred as milk output per cow actually increased 25 percent over the same period (ONE). Cereals (rice and corn), sugar cane, tropical fruits, and vegetables accounted for 84 percent of harvested area in 2013.

Cuba's field crop yields, harvested area and production have varied widely over the past decade. Corn yields averaged 47 bushels/acre in 2013, compared to 160 bushels/acre in the United States. These yields, however, were up 20 percent from 41 bushels/acre in the period from 2003-08. Harvested area for corn declined from 556,000 acres in 2010 to 440,000 acres in 2013. In 2013, Cuba rice yields averaged 3,000 pounds per acre, compared to 7,400 in the United States. Harvested area for rice was down five percent to 489,000 acres. Rice production was up in 2013 to 677,000 metric tons, however, nearly 20 percent more than 2010.

Because of poor soil conditions, high humidity, timing and amounts of rainfall, high insect infestation and lack of pesticide or biological controls, Cuba's ability to produce grain and oilseed crops is limited and likely to remain so over the long term. According to FAO, 42 percent of Cuba's agricultural land is affected by medium to highly erodible soils. Poor drainage and low fertility affect 40 to 44 percent of soils, while 70 percent experience low organic matter. As a result, Cuba will remain one of the top grain and oilseed product markets in the Caribbean region.

International Visitors in Cuba

A record 3.0 million international visitors traveled to Cuba in 2014, up from 2.0 million in 2004. Slightly more than 90,000 international visitors were U.S. business representatives and other approved categories. Revenue from international visitors is a major source of foreign exchange for the government of Cuba (GOC), ranked third behind technical services and remittances. It is also an important source of income for Cubans working in tourism such as wait staff, taxi drivers and tour operators. This revenue was equivalent to 57 percent of all merchandise exports in 2009 and 28 percent of the balance of all services trade for 2007. Further, as Cuban tourism earnings increased by six percent from 2006 to 2008, U.S. exports doubled. As earnings from tourism declined 11 percent in 2009, U.S. exports fell by 25 percent. The potential increases in U.S. food and agricultural exports to Cuba due to increased travel range from $48 million to $366 million/year, creating up to 5,500 new jobs, these estimates include only the additional spending by new U.S. visitors to Cuba (Rosson, Adcock and Manthei).

Changes implemented by the GOC in April 2008 allow Cubans to stay at some tourist hotels and resorts (Dominican Today). Many of the 4 and 5 star facilities are out of the price range of most locals who earn the equivalent of about $20/month. During the low season of 2009 (August), however, some of the 2 and 3 star hotels in Varadero, Cuba's major tourist beach resort area, were booking one-week stays to locals for around $200/week (Global Post). With about 60 percent of Cubans having access to hard currency (Calgary Herald) either from remittances, factory and farm bonuses, or tips, these 'new' tourists, are creating some additional demand for U.S. food products.

While many other forces also influenced U.S. exports, and cause-effect may be debatable, there does appear to be a fairly strong linkage between the amount of money Cuba earns from visits to the island and the amount of food it can afford to import from the United States and other suppliers. USDA estimated in 2008 that the proportion of imported foods supplying the tourist trade in Cuba was between 25 and 33 percent. CNAS estimates indicate that the U.S. share of the Cuban food market for international visitors is about 40 percent, implying that each tourism dollar spent in Cuba generates an additional $0.10 to $0.13 in U.S. food exports needed to supply the Cuban tourist trade.

In conclusion, the Cuban market for U.S. food and agricultural exports has potential for growth. From modest beginnings, the market has shown strong growth at times, but also weakness. Our estimates indicate that U.S. food and agricultural exports to Cuba have the potential to exceed $1.0 billion annually. These additional exports would support the creation of 6,000 new jobs throughout the U.S. economy. For this potential economic impact to realized, however, several challenges lie ahead. First, income growth and economic prosperity for Cubans is needed. Second, infrastructure improvement and investment will be necessary to improve the efficiency of existing supply chain and the creation of new cold chains to handle processed foods. Finally, policies and regulations that facilitate trade, and that are transparent and consistent are an absolute necessity. Open trade would certainly lead to more rapid growth, but absent free trade, less regulation of financing, the use of letters of credit and improvements in banking conditions in Cuba would stimulate U.S. export growth. Thank you again for allowing me to testify on the opportunities and challenges affecting U.S. agriculture trade in Cuba.

References

Calgary Herald. Cubans Allowed to Stay at Tourist Hotels. March 31, 2008. www.canada.com/calgaryherald.

Carrillo, Venus. Tourism in Cuba, So Far So Good, OnCuba, Fuego Media Group, March 15, 2015.

Central Intelligence Agency of the United States. World Factbook, Cuba and the Dominical Republic, April 2015.

Cuba Standard. March 19, 2014. Cubastandard.com.

Dominican Today. Cubans Can Stay in Hotels. April 1, 2008. www.dominican today. com.

Food and Agriculture Organization of the United Nations. Land Resources Information Systems in the Caribbean. 2000.

Foreign Agricultural Service, USDA. Global Agricultural Trading System (GATS), online database. www.fas.usda.gov.

Global Post. *At Cuban Resorts, the of Tourism Apartheid.* August 10, 2009. www.globalpost.com.

Office of Global Analysis, Foreign Agricultural Service, USDA. *Cuba's Food and Agriculture Situation Report,* March 2008.

Oficina Nacional de Estadísticas (ONE). Republic of Cuba, 2008 and 2015 Series. Located at www.one.cu.

Rosson, C. Parr, Flynn J. Adcock and Eric Manthei. *Estimated Economic Impacts of the Travel Restriction Reform and Export Enhancement Act of 2010* by the Center for North American Studies, Texas A&M AgriLife Research, Texas A&M University, submitted for the record to the House Committee on Agriculture, United States House of Representatives, March 11, 2010. www.cubaweather.org/cu.

In: Agricultural Trade Between the U.S. and Cuba ISBN: 978-1-63484-430-7
Editor: Lana Valdez

Chapter 10

CUBA: FOOD AND AGRICULTURAL IMPORT REGULATIONS AND STANDARDS - NARRATIVE*

Omar Gonzalez

REPORT HIGHLIGHTS

The United States allows for the export of agricultural products to Cuba in conformity with the Trade Sanctions Reform and Export Enhancement Act of 2000. U.S. suppliers willing to navigate a detailed set of U.S. regulatory controls related to exporting to Cuba will find that the island is fairly receptive to U.S. products. This report provides information on Cuba's regulatory environment as it relates to U.S. agricultural exports. Cuban requirements related to product labeling, sanitary product registration, and export documentation generally are similar to those of other Latin American countries. However, the key difference in exporting to Cuba, compared to other countries in the region, is that all U.S. agricultural exports must be channeled through one Cuban government agency, ALIMPORT.

---

* This is an edited, reformatted and augmented version of Global Agricultural Information Network Report Number CB1416, issued by the USDA Foreign Agricultural Service, December 10, 2014.

DISCLAIMER

This report was prepared by the Caribbean Basin Agricultural Trade Office of the USDA/Foreign Agricultural Service in Miami, Florida, for U.S. exporters of domestic food and agricultural products. While every possible care was taken in the preparation of this report, information provided may not be completely accurate either because policies have changed since its preparation, or because clear and consistent information about these policies was not available. It is highly recommended that U.S. exporters verify the full set of import requirements with their foreign customers, who are normally best equipped to research such matters with local authorities, before any goods are shipped. FINAL IMPORT APPROVAL OF ANY PRODUCT IS SUBJECT TO THE IMPORTING COUNTRY'S RULES AND REGULATIONS AS INTERPRETED BY BORDER OFFICIALS AT THE TIME OF PRODUCT ENTRY.

SECTION I. GENERAL FOOD LAWS

The government-operated Empresa Comercializadora de Alimentos (ALIMPORT) is the sole buying agency for U.S. agricultural products. ALIMPORT negotiates for client Cuban entities and handles all purchasing, documentation and logistics. Other Cuban agencies may import from non-U.S. sources, but in the case of the United States, ALIMPORT is the exclusive negotiating and procurement party.

The Ministry of Agriculture is responsible for regulating imports of animals and animal products, as well as imports of plants and plant products. Live animals and animal product imports are regulated by the Ministry's Institute of Veterinary Medicine (IMV) and are subject to regulations of Decree 137 of 1993. Imports of live plants and plant products are regulated by the National Center for Plant Health (CNSV) and are subject to regulations set forth in Resolution 366 of 1990 and Resolution 435 of 1994.

Similarly, the Cuban Ministry of Health's Institute of Nutrition and Food Safety (INHA) is responsible for regulating imports of consumer-ready foods. USDA export certificates are required for bulk grain and meat products, particularly for fresh, frozen, and canned meats. Enforcement is carried out mostly at the port of entry, where scrutiny can be intense and at the importer warehouse level. Enforcement at the retail level is minimal.

U.S. exporters should keep in mind that USDA officials did not contact Cuban government officials to prepare this report due to legal or policy restrictions on such contacts. Therefore, we encourage U.S. exporters to work closely with the importer and/or the Cuban government to fully verify import requirements for agricultural goods.

SECTION II. FOOD ADDITIVE REGULATIONS

Cuban law does not cite any major restrictions on additives. Thus, if the additive is recognized as being suitable for human consumption, particularly by Codex standards, it is considered acceptable by the Cuban Ministry of Health.

U.S. exporters can obtain a complete list of additives that are acceptable to the Cuban Ministry of Health directly from the Ministry's Institute of Nutrition and Food Safety (INHA) listed in Appendix I. U.S. exporters wishing to introduce a food product containing a new additive into Cuba should contact the above specified agency and be prepared to submit the proper documentation/samples for scientific analysis prior to approval.

SECTION III. PESTICIDE AND OTHER CONTAMINANTS

The Ministry of Health is the agency charged with regulating pesticide/contaminant residues in foodstuffs. The Ministry uses its own list of approved products and acceptable tolerance levels for each. U.S. exporters may obtain a copy of these lists by contacting INHA. As a general rule of thumb, Codex maximum residue limits are acceptable for most foodstuffs. If a pesticide/contaminant is suspected of affecting the food supply or producing illness, the Ministry of Health will remove it from its list of approved products until it can conduct the proper analysis and determine its impact on the consumer.

SECTION IV. PACKAGING AND CONTAINER REQUIREMENTS

Cuba has no special Municipal Waste Disposal Laws or product recycling regulations. The manufacturer has the flexibility to use any packaging material as long as it is acceptable for use with food products. PVC and similar materials are fully acceptable in Cuba.

SECTION V. LABELING REQUIREMENTS

All food products are required to be labeled in Spanish. Multilingual labels are acceptable as long as Spanish is one of the languages used on the label. Following is the information required by Cuban law on all prepackaged food product labels:

1. Name of the food product;
2. Country of origin;
3. Commercial brand name;
4. Name and address of the manufacturer;
5. Ingredients and additives;
6. Net content and drained weight;
7. Instructions for use;
8. Storage instructions; and
9. Date of manufacture or lot number/code and expiration date.

In addition to the above mandatory labeling requirements, Cuban authorities may also refer to internationally accepted Codex Alimentarius (Codex) standards if discrepancies with foreign labels exist. Codex, also known as the "food code," is a set of scientifically-based and globally-recognized standards, codes of practice, guidelines and recommendations for food products.

Standard U.S. product labels are generally acceptable. However, stick-on labels may be required to comply with the Spanish language requirement or any of the nine labeling requirements listed above that are not specified on the U.S. product label. It is recommended that any stick-on labels be affixed to the product prior to arrival in Cuba, so that the product is fully compliant at the port of entry, and the customs clearance process is not delayed. As mentioned earlier, the port of entry is the main point of enforcement. In addition, while stick-on labels will fulfill import requirements in the short term, U.S. companies seeking to export food products to Cuba over the long run should label their products according to Cuban requirements without the use of stick-on labels (to avoid any possible complications at the port of entry).

Cuban regulations do not specifically address labeling requirements for samples or institutional-packed products for the food service industry. However, in the case of institutional packed products, health authorities normally do not expect to see all the information required on labels of retail products. The boxes or cases in which institutional products are shipped must be labeled with the name or description of the product and with the product size. The products themselves should be individually labeled with the same information as well. However, given that the end use of institutional packed products cannot always be guaranteed, it is recommended that they be labeled the same as retail products when possible.

Cuba has no specific standards regarding irradiated food products. U.S. standards on this subject are acceptable.

SECTION VI. OTHER SPECIFIC STANDARDS

U.S. exporters should ascertain whether their products will require a zoo sanitary import permit (for animal products) or a phytosanitary import permit (for plant products) prior to exporting any agricultural product to Cuba. These permits, issued by the Cuban Ministry of Agriculture's IMV or CNSV, are normally obtained by the importer. The Cuban government requires the appropriate zoo/phyto-sanitary import permit from the importing party before any trade contract is executed. In order to obtain such permits, the following is usually required:

1. Commercial name of the product;
2. Scientific name of the product (if applicable);
3. Use of the product;
4. Method of transportation into Cuba;
5. Country of origin; and
6. Country from which the product is being delivered to Cuba.

In the case of meat products, a visit by a Cuban Ministry official to the farm and/or processing facility from which the products originate may be required prior to granting a zoo sanitary import permit. Any plant product posing a risk to plant health will require a phytosanitary import permit. Such is the case for live plants or parts of plants, seeds, animal feeds, forestry products, products for industrial use such as cotton, tobacco, and medicinal plants and herbs. For the most part, processed consumer-ready food products are not subject to such requirements by the Ministry of Agriculture. However, U.S. exporters are urged to verify the need for any sanitary permits from the Ministry of Agriculture.

Also, all U.S. exporting companies must be registered with the government of Cuba prior to shipping any products to Cuba. Procedures have been streamlined and consist of sending the following documentation to ALIMPORT (see Appendix I for contact information):

1. Company name, address, short history, officers, and any other information demonstrating bona fides of the exporting company;
2. Technical specifications of the product(s);
3. Certificate of free sale;
4. Phytosanitary or health certificate.

Travelers carrying food samples into Cuba are required to declare the products to Cuban Customs. Be advised that Customs may request additional authorization/documentation by the appropriate regulatory agency for products subject to special import requirements (i.e., meat products). As a general rule of thumb, the declared value of the merchandise should read "No Commercial Value" in the case of samples. Customs rulings taken against travelers or their luggage may be appealed. Initial claims should be made to the Chief of the Customs unit where the ruling was originally made. Claims can be escalated to the next highest level if need be.

Although compliance with health standards is verified mostly at the port of entry and at the importer warehouse level, the Cuban government does exercise some control, albeit on a very limited basis, at the retail level. When random inspections by health officials uncover irregularities such as spoiled product or product past its expiration, the product is usually confiscated. Store managers may be penalized depending on the severity of the violation. The same applies at the wholesale level, except in this case the scrutiny is more intense. At the wholesale level the penalties for violations are also higher. In addition to product confiscation and fines, penalties may also include total removal of the product from the island and temporary suspension of import privileges for the particular item in question.

SECTION VII. FACILITY AND PRODUCT REGISTRATION REQUIREMENTS

Prior to the shipment of any U.S. consumer-oriented food products to Cuba, U.S. exporters must ensure that their product undergoes sanitary product registration with INHA. Because ALIMPORT is the sole buying agency for U.S. products, they usually facilitate the sanitary product registration procedure with INHA. The following is required for purposes of sanitary product registration:

1. Company name;
2. Product;
3. Commercial name;
4. Name of the manufacturer;
5. Country of origin;
6. Physical and chemical specifications of the product;
7. Composition (list of ingredients);
8. Product label (must conform with Cuban Standard NC108:2001 or CODEX STAN 1-1985);
9. Date marking (date of minimum durability);
10. Packaging;
11. Food Additives;
12. Limits of metal contaminants;
13. Limits of microbiological contaminants;
14. Other contaminants;
15. Storage instructions;
16. Information required to decipher the lot code (if applicable);
17. Certificates
    a) Certificate of free sale;
    b) Operating certificate or sanitary license of the manufacturing establishment;
18. Instructions for use (and any other pertinent information about the product).

In addition to the above, three product samples are also required. There are no requirements for sample sizes for testing. However, U.S. exporters should use common sense in providing samples in quantities or sizes ample enough for laboratory analysis. Registration usually takes about 15 days from the time that all the documents and samples have been received.

SECTION VIII. OTHER CERTIFICATION AND TESTING REQUIREMENTS

For information related to Cuba's requirements for meat products exported from the United States, see USDA's Food Safety and Inspection Service's Export Library (www.fsis.usda.gov/Regulations_&_Policies/Cuba_Requirements/index.asp).

For information on Cuba's requirements for live animals exported from the United States, see USDA's Animal and Plant Health Inspection Service website (www.aphis.usda.gov/regulations/vs/iregs/animals/animalcuba.shtml).

Information on exporting animal products to Cuba such dairy products and pet foods can be found at http://www.aphis.usda.gov/regulations/vs/iregs/products/product cuba.shtml.

Vitamins and nutritional products are considered pharmaceutical in nature, and they are not sold in supermarkets or retail food stores. These types of products are sold in pharmacies only.

SECTION IX. IMPORT PROCEDURES

Despite some liberalizing moves in the last four years, the Cuban government maintains a strict monopoly on foreign trade. Customs entry must be handled by an authorized Customs Agent contracted and acting in the name of a Cuban state-controlled company legally allowed to import a given category of product. A list of such agents can be obtained from the Cuban Customs Administration (see Appendix I for contact information). The entry process begins with submittal of a customs merchandise declaration. This declaration must be accompanied by the following documents:

1. Shipping documents (original bill of lading, export certification where applicable, etc.)

2. Commercial invoice (original)
3. Packing list (original)
4. Certificate of Origin
5. Phytosanitary/zoo sanitary and fumigation certificates in the case of wood

All documents must be translated into Spanish. Cuban Customs offers some leeway in terms of documentation. For instance, Pro-forma invoices are temporarily accepted. Importers are also allowed to submit Customs declarations in advance of shipment arrivals, and make temporary or incomplete declarations when all the information necessary for clearance is not readily available. However, a commitment to submit a complete declaration and all the remaining documentation is required.

Shipments are inspected and cleared at three different levels. At the first level, merchandise goes through any one of three channels: green, orange or red. In the green channel, neither the documents nor the merchandise are inspected. In the orange channel, the documents are reviewed to determine if a physical inspection of the merchandise is required. In the red channel, clearance is granted only after the merchandise has been physically inspected. In the second clearance level, the documentation is reviewed again to determine if any errors in classification, valuation, or duty assessment may exist. The third and final level of clearance involves post clearance inspections, which may take place up to five years after the merchandise is imported into the country. Customs may apply administrative sanctions to any importer or customs agents found to be negligent or to exercise malicious intent.

Customs clearance time may vary depending on the volume of cargo entering Cuba at any given time, and the number of documents required for specific merchandise. The entire process may take one to three weeks depending on the effectiveness of the Customs Broker. Information contained in the Bill of Lading and pertaining to the consignee must be complete and accurate. Discrepancies in this regard will most likely delay the clearance process.

Decisions by Customs officials to reject merchandise may be appealed. Depending on the grounds for rejection, the head of the Customs Department or the Minister of Health will have the final say on whether or not merchandise can be imported into the country.

Applicable laws governing Customs procedures include:

1. Joint Resolution No. 1 Ministry of Finances and Prices – Ministry of Foreign Trade and Foreign Investment
2. Customs Duties of the Republic of Cuba – 2014 Update
3. Decree No. 162: Customs Law of the Republic of Cuba (May 1996)
4. Decree No. 207: Customs Administrative Infractions (May 1996)

Cuba uses the nomenclature of the harmonized system up to 8 digits. Duties for most favored nations (WTO members and those with bilateral agreements with Cuba) average 10.3 percent. However, imports from the United States do not receive most favored nation treatment. Non-most favored nation duties currently average 16.6 percent. For more information on the subject, please refer to the Cuban Tariff Schedule which is available on the Cuban Customs Administration website (see Appendix III.B.).

SECTION X. COPYRIGHT AND/OR TRADEMARK LAWS

All trademarks and brand names registered in Cuba are protected under Cuban law. The main legislation governing trademark registration is Decree No. 203-99: Trademarks and Other Distinctive Signs (December 24, 1999). Trademark registration with the Cuban Office of Industrial Property (OCPI) is voluntary. U.S. exporters shipping their products to Cuba are advised to make every effort to register their trademarks and brand names in Cuba in order to obtain protection against infringement. A trademark registration is valid for ten years and may be renewed indefinitely for successive ten year periods. A list of registration fees is available on the OCPI website (see Appendix III.B). U.S. exporters should be aware that although they may own the trademark for their product in the United States, this does not necessarily prevent someone else from registering it in Cuba. Legally established firms in Cuba, domestic and foreign, can register a trademark through their legal representative, a designated representative, or an official agent (see Appendix II.B for a list of such agents). Foreign firms not legally established in Cuba must conduct all business with the Cuban Office of Industrial Property through an official agent. For further information on the trademark registration process, U.S. exporters should consult with an official agent.

Section XI. U.S. Export Controls

The U.S. Department of Commerce's Bureau of Industry and Security (BIS) regulates exports to Cuba. Any person seeking to ship any goods, including samples, from the United States to Cuba directly or indirectly, must first obtain authorization from BIS. The U.S. Treasury Department's Office of Foreign Assets Control (OFAC) administers the Cuban Assets Control Regulations that regulate travel to Cuba and use of dollars by travelers in Cuba. Contact information for both BIS and OFAC can found in Appendix II.A.

Appendix I. Government Regulatory Key Agency Contacts

For general purchasing, documentation and logistics issues related to the importation of bulk and intermediate U.S. agricultural products:

ALIMPORT
Infanta #16, 3er Piso
Vedado, Plaza
La Habana, Cuba
Tel: 011 (537) 873-2014
Fax: 011 (537) 873-3151
E-mail: alimport@alimport.com.cu

For general purchasing, documentation and logistics issues related to the importation of processed U.S. agricultural products

ALIMPORT MID
Calle 8 No. 508
E/5ta y 5ta B Playa
Tel: 011 (537) 204-1395/1274
Fax: 011 (537) 204-1395

For sanitary registration of food products and other food safety issues:

Instituto de Nutrición e Higiene de los Alimentos (Institute of Nutrition and Food Safety)
Ministerio de Salud Pública (Ministry of Public Health)
Infanta No. 1158 entre Llinás y Clavel
Centro Habana
Ciudad de la Habana, Cuba CP 10300
Tel: 011 (537) 878-1429, 878-5919, 870-5531 to 34
Fax: 011 (537) 833-8313
E-mail: dirinha@infomed.sld.cu & dsi@sinha.sld.cu

For labeling and other standards:

Oficina Nacional de Normalización (National Standards Office)
Ministerio de Ciencia, Tecnología y Medio Ambiente (Ministry of Science, Technology and the Environment)
Calle E No. 261 entre 11 y 13 Vedado
Plaza, La Habana 10400
Tel: 011 (537) 830-0803, 830-0732 ext. 12, 18 &46 830-0825
Fax: 011 (537) 836-8048
E mail: nc@ncnorma.cu

For live animals and animal product import requirements:

Instituto de Medicina Veterinaria (Institute of Veterinary Medicine)
Ministerio de Agricultura (Ministry of Agriculture)
Calle 12 #355 E/15 y 17, Plaza de la Revolución
Ciudad de la Habana, Cuba CP 10400
Tel: 011 (537) 833-7077
Fax: n/a
E-mail: rbescofet@infomed.sld.cu, pssantos@infomed.sld.cu, egmerlo@ infomed.sld.cu

For plant and plant product import requirements:

Centro Nacional de Sanidad Vegetal (National Plant Health Center)
Ministerio de Agricultura (Ministry of Agriculture)
Ayuntamiento No. 231

e/Lombillo y San Pedro, Plaza de la Revolución
Ciudad de la Habana, Cuba
Tel: 011 (537) 879-1339, 870-0925, 881-5089
Fax: 011 (537) 870-3277
E-mail: cnsv@ceniai.inf.cu,
director@sanidadvegetal.cu

Other:

Oficina Cubana de la Propiedad Industrial (Cuban Office of Industrial Property)
Ministerio de Ciencia, Tecnología y Medio Ambiente (Ministry of Science, Technology & the Environment)
Calle Picota No. 15, Entre Luz y Acosta
Habana Vieja, Apartado 2180 Habana 2, C.P. 10200
Ciudad de la Habana, Cuba
Tel: 011 (537) 862-4379, 861-3602, 862-9771, 866-0557 to 59, 862-4395
Fax: 011 (537) 866-5610
E-mail: ocpi@ocpi.cu, info@ocpi.cu

Aduana General de la República de Cuba (Cuban Customs Administration) Calle 6, Esquina a 39, Plaza Revolución
Ciudad de la Habana, Cuba CP 10600
Tel: 011 (537) 855-5466 to 71 ext. 227, 883-8282, 883-7575, 881-9732
E-mail: publico@agr.aduana.cu

Appendix II. Other Import Specialist Technical Contacts

A. U.S. Government Contacts

Caribbean Basin Agricultural Trade Office
Foreign Agricultural Service
U.S. Department of Agriculture
909 SE 1st. Ave, Suite 720
Miami, FL 33131
Tel: (305) 536-5300

Fax: (305) 536-7577
E-mail: atocaribbeanbasin@fas.usda.gov
Website: http://www.cbato.fas.usda.gov

Michael T. Henney, Director
Omar González, Agricultural Marketing Specialist
Graciela Juelle, Agricultural Marketing Assistant

Office of Exporter Services
Bureau of Industry and Security U.S. Department of Commerce Washington, D.C.
Tel: (202) 482-4811
Fax: (202) 482-2927
Website: www.bis.doc.gov

Office of Foreign Assets Control
U.S. Department of the Treasury
Treasury Annex
1500 Pennsylvania Avenue, NW
Washington, DC 20220
Tel: (800) 540-6322
Fax on Demand Service: (202) 622-0077
Website: www.treas.gov/offices/enforcement/ofac/index.shtml

B. Non-U.S. Government Contacts

Accredited Customs Agents:

ADESA
Avenida del Puerto E/LFCC y Pote
Habana Vieja
Tel: 011 (537) 794-4041, 794-4396 ext. 258

AEROVARADERO S.A
Carretera Wajay Km. 1 Aijm, Boyeros
Tel: 011 (537) 266-4118, 649-0297
Fax: 011 (537) 266-4118

*ALMACENES UNIVERSALES S.A.*_Fabrica #45 E/Aspuru y LFCC
Habana Vieja
Tel: 011 (537) 690-2367, 698-7344 Fax: 011 (537) 690-2341

CONSIG.MARITIMA CARIBEŇA
5ta. Avenida No. 4001 E/40 y 42 Playa
Tel: 011 (537) 204-1226 Fax: 011 (537) 204-1227

CUBACONTROL S.A.
Calle Conill Esquina 26 #580 Plaza Tel: 011 (537) 855-5737, 855-5720

CUBANACAN EXPRESS S.A.
5ta-A #66 No. 6223, esq. 66, Playa
Tel: 011 (537) 204-7848 Fax: 011 (537) 204-2499

CUBAPACK INTERNATIONAL, S.A. Calle 22 #4115 E/41 y 47, Playa
Tel: 011 (537) 204-1774 Fax: 011 (537) 204-2226

EMP. DE SERV. LOG., LOGIDEX Loma No 674 E/Colon y Lombillo, Plaza Telefax: 011 (537) 855-5439

*EMPRESA CONSG. MAMBISA*_San Jose #65 E/Prado y Zulueta Habana Vieja
Tel: 011 (537) 862-2061/65 Ext. 144 Fax: 011 (537) 866-8111

EMPRESA CORREOS DE CUBA Desamparados #166 E/Habana y Compostela Habana Vieja
Tel: 011 (537) 861-2667, 862-9360 Fax: 011 (537) 861-2667

MUSEO NACIONAL DE BELLAS ARTES
Trocadero, Zulucta y Monserrate
Habana Vieja
Tel: 011 (537) 863-9484, 861-3857 ext. 11 Fax: 011 (537) 862-9626

*PALACIO DE CONVENCIONES*_Calle-146/11 y 13 Rpart, Playa Tel: 011 (537) 208-6111 2080653 Fax: 011 (537) 208-6111

SERVITALLY
Desamparados S/N Esq. Compostela Habana Vieja

Tel: 011 (537) 866-9138, 6426156 Fax: 011 (537) 642-6156

TECNOTEX
Ave del Puerto, "Edificio La Marina" E/Justiz y Obrapia
Habana Vieja
Tel: 011 (537) 861-7692, 861-3536, 861-064
Fax: 011 (537) 66-6270

TRANSCARGO
Fabrica No.54 E/Aspuru y Linea Ferroc.
Habana Vieja
Tel: 011 (537) 690 5409, 794 1741
Fax: 011 (537) 698-6451

Official agents specializing in trademark registration:

BUFETE INTERNACIONAL, CONSULTORES DE MARCAS Y PATENTES
Casa Matriz
5ta. Avenida No. 4002
Esquina 40, Playa
Ciudad de la Habana
Tel: 011 (537) 204-5126, 204-5127, 204-5736, 204-5737
Fax: 011 (537) 204-5125
E-mail: marcas@bufeteinternacional.cu
CLAIM, S.A.
Lamparilla # 2, Lonja del Comercio, Oficina 6
Habana Vieja, Ciudad de La Habana CP 10100
Tel: 011 (537) 33-0743, 33-0755, 866-0743, 866-0755 Fax: 011 (537) 33-0746
E-mail: dirmarpat@claim.com.cu & claim@claim.com.cu

CONSULTORIA JURIDICA INTERNACIONAL
Calle 16 No. 314, entre 3ra y 5ta. Avenida, Miramar Playa, Ciudad de La Habana
Teléfonos: 011 (537) 204-2490, 204-2469
Fax: 011 (537) 204-2303
E-mail: cji@cji.co.cu

LEX, S.A. SERVICIOS JURIDICOS DE MARCAS Y PATENTES
Calle 1ra No. 1001, Esquina 10, Miramar
Playa, Ciudad de la Habana
Tel: 011 (537) 204-9093
Fax: 011 (537) 204-9533
E-mail: lexsa@lex-sa.cu

BUFETE ESPECIALIZADO
Calle 23 No. 501, Esquina a J. Vedado, Plaza de la Revolución
Ciudad de la Habana
Tel: 011 (537) 832-6813, 832-6024
Fax: 011 (537) 833-2159
E-mail: besnet@ceniai.inf.cu

APPENDIX III. USEFUL WEBSITES/LINKS

A. U.S. Government Websites/Links

1. http://www.fas.usda.gov/sites/default/files/2014-04/schedulebeligible commodities06-28-06.pdf - USDA list of commodities (agricultural, fish & forestry) eligible for shipment to Cuba.
2. http://www.bis.doc.gov/ - U.S. Department of Commerce, Bureau of Industry and Security website. Information on exporting agricultural commodities to Cuba can be found at http://www.bis.doc. gov/index. php/policy-guidance/country-guidance/sanctioned-destinations/cuba.
3. http://www.treasury.gov/resource-center/sanctions/Programs/pages/ cuba.aspx - U.S. Department of the Treasury, Office of Foreign Assets Control website. This site offers an overview of Cuban assets control regulations and guidelines and information on the Cuba sanctions program, including information on rules related to use of dollars by travelers and permitted travel. A list of OFAC-Authorized providers of air, travel and remittance forwarding services can be found at: http://www.treasury.gov/resource-center/sanctions/Prog rams/Docu ments/cuba_tsp.pdf
4. http://www.state.gov/r/pa/ei/bgn/2886.htm - U.S. Department of State fact sheet on U.S. relations with Cuba. This site offers general background information on the subject.

5. http://havana.usint.gov - U.S. Interests Section in Havana website. This site offers information on U.S. citizen services as well as USG and non-USG resources.
6. https://www.cia.gov/library/publications/the-world-factbook/geos/cu.html - Central Intelligence Agency's World Factbook website. The World Factbook provides general information on Cuba and other countries around the world.

B. Non-U.S. Government Websites/Links

The websites listed below are provided for the reader's convenience; USDA does NOT in any way endorse, guarantee the accuracy of, or necessarily concur with the information contained in these websites.

1. http://www1.lanic.utexas.edu/la/cb/cuba/ - The University of Texas' Latin American Network Information Center (LANIC) provides a comprehensive listing of websites related to Cuba. English & Spanish.
2. http://www.nconline.cubaindustria.cu/entrada_english.asp - Cuban Standards On-line. This site provides a catalog of Cuban standards which can be searched for free. Downloading is available to subscribers for a fee. Spanish & English.
3. http://www.aduana.co.cu - Cuban Customs Administration website. This site offers detailed information on Customs clearance legislation, requirements, procedures, accredited Customs agents, and other useful information. Cuba's duty schedule can be viewed at: http://www.aduana.co.cu/images/stories/aduana/comercial/arancel-2014/goe-58.rar (RAR compressed archive file requiring software to extract or unzip content). Spanish & English Section.

INDEX

#

A

B

C

F

G

H

I

J

K

L

S

T

U

V

W

Y